THE ARMY, DEPRESSIO

By Victoria Pren

PROLOGUE

I was ready to die.

I *wanted* to die.

It was Christmas Eve – there were presents under the tree in the living room and my little girl Abi was asleep in her bedroom upstairs, but it didn't matter.

None of it mattered anymore.

In the semi-dark of the living room, lit only by the sparkling lights of the tree, I took my little girl's school tie and wrapped it around my arm, the sound of Jon Bon Jovi singing softly in the background.

Hey man I'm alive, I'm takin' each day and night at a time

I'm feelin' like a Monday but someday I'll be Saturday night

I'd woken up that morning like every other morning. I was sick. I had taken so many drugs the day before that I'd woken up and vomited. This had become a regular occurrence.

I had borrowed money to fund Abi's Christmas presents. I got credit from a catalogue lady; you know, those who sell vouchers for the high street stores but on high interest credit. I'd also got a door step loan. I think in total I had borrowed £500, but for that pleasure I now owed over £2500 with its interest and the time it would take for me to pay it off. With that debt – along with my Council tax arrears, my gas and electric arrears, my water bill arrears, my Sky having been cut off along with my phone line because that was also in arrears, my red letter bills from previous lenders, and also my ever-increasing drug bills – my debts had mounted up enormously.

It was time to be honest – I now owed over *fifteen thousand pounds*.

And while the council might understand, I knew the drug dealers most definitely would *not*.

How the hell had I gotten so bad?

I just couldn't see a way out. I tried to paint a smile on my face for Abi's sake but that night when she'd gone to bed I'd hit the bottle bad and I'd sobbed uncontrollably.

I'd then contacted a different drug dealer – one I didn't owe any money to, and who I actually considered to be a friend. This time when I spoke to this person I'd asked if I could have 5 bags of heroin and a needle. Within an hour the doorbell rang and my order was ready. My drug dealer had come in for a little while and was asking why I was changing my order (he knew I only ever had cocaine from the other dealer) and he'd asked if I was sure about what I was doing. I'd explained I had never injected before and I wasn't sure how to do it, so he'd taught me the basics. We spoke for an hour but strangely this was the first time payment was not even mentioned. I think the dealer knew deep down what I was about to do and so it wasn't brought up. With that he'd left, leaving me alone once more.

I hadn't even bothered taking my stolen turkey out the freezer. What the hell was the point? I knew Abi was going at lunch time on Christmas Day to her Dad's and that meant I would be spending most of Christmas alone. Wow, great fun. Depressed and alone on Christmas Day, how perfect. The thought was too much to bear.

I couldn't even watch TV on the run-up to Christmas because every single advert was full of happy families around a big dinner table happily singing Christmas songs whilst tucking into a feast. Me, well I didn't even have a proper table – I'd sold my good one to buy drugs.

I'd written Abi a goodbye letter. I knew the past few months I had been a horrendous Mummy and I knew she deserved better. I knew deep down she needed to live with her Dad but giving her up full time would have killed me. In my letter I explained how much I loved her and since the day she was born all I had done was fight to survive but I no longer had it in me. I was sorry for being a let-down but I knew I could do a better job watching over her from afar. I had pushed the letter under her pillow and kissed her on the head, then watched her sleep for a few minutes. I hadn't been able to stay longer – the pain was killing me. I needed it over. So with that, I'd closed her bedroom door and headed down the stairs.

And now I was on the couch, her tie around my arm, waiting for the heroin to come to the boil.

Finally it was ready, and I turned off the Christmas lights. I didn't want to see them anymore; there was no sparkle left.

I drew the heroin up into the syringe, watching in fascination as the fluid that would soon kill me filled the plastic vacuum.

I pulled the school tie tight around my arm and hunted for a vein. There was no need to disinfect anything; I wouldn't be alive long enough to suffer from infection.

I found a vein, Bon Jovi still ringing in my ears.

And Tuesday just might go my way

It can't get worse than yesterday

Thursdays, Fridays ain't been kind

But somehow I'll survive

I clutched a family photo to my chest with my left hand, the needle held in my right as tears ran freely down my cheeks.

Goodbye Abi.

I put the needle to my vein and pierced the skin, the sudden stab of pain making everything so clear, so real.

And – with no other way out – I started to press down hard on the syringe and inject the heroin into my bloodstream.

How had I arrived at that fateful point in my life?

What had led up to that terrible Christmas Eve?

That is my story, one that I hope you will find interesting but that I hope you never have to live through yourself.

If it can be, let my story act as a warning – and, in its own way – as an inspiration.

CHAPTER 1: SCHOOL DAYS

Sometimes I wonder where my life would have taken me if I hadn't touched drugs. I definitely know I would never in a million years have joined the army; and if I hadn't joined the army I wouldn't have had my children. That is a thought I cannot fathom.

My children saved me.

My name is Vikki. There is nothing special about me, I am an ordinary mother and an ordinary wife who has lived a not so ordinary life to get to the ordinary. I was born in October 1983 in Scarborough North Yorkshire.

My mother and father separated soon after my birth and so my mother and I moved and I was brought up in Inverness, Scotland. My childhood was not the best, but it certainly wasn't the worst either. In the grand scheme of things there are millions of children who have endured far worse than me. I cannot complain, I always knew underneath it all, I was loved. To me that is everything.

From a young age I watched my mother battle alcohol addiction and although I never understood it, I always feared it. I saw the devastating effect it had on my mum and it scared me. I never understood mental illness either and at such a young age I wasn't sure I wanted too. Little did I know then, that this mental illness/addiction battle I was witnessing now on someone else was the easy part. For living with it is far, far worse.

I enjoyed primary school and to a certain degree I enjoyed secondary school but by the age of 12, I had lost count of the number of times I had moved house and this played a part in my confidence at school. My first years of my life were spent with my mum, step dad and little sister. Sounds quite idyllic but in reality my childhood was pretty chaotic with family arguments and house moves. I always felt unsettled and this has continued throughout my whole life. My mum met a new man not long after my tenth birthday and I firmly believe my start in life would have been very much different if it was not for this. It was safe to say we did not get on. I cannot blame him entirely, I was quite a moody teenager and he was very set in his ways so together we just clashed. I was always bubbly at school and at home I always seemed miserable. Looking back now the signs were there that this could have been the start of a mood disorder.

I was always quite sporty as a teenager and I enjoyed keeping fit. I never smoked, even though my mother and her partner smoked like chimneys. I hated it. Typical teenagers in school would go and buy 20p cigarettes at break times but I was always too busy goofing around and being the joker. It took my mind off my own issues. I knew I was a bit odd looking at school – long skinny twig-like legs, goofy teeth, frizzy hair and freckles. I knew people laughed at me and so my only coping mechanism was to join them. My daily break time and lunchtime routine at school was to join in taking the piss out of myself. It was easier that way and it helped me fit in with the cool kids. I certainly didn't want to go home and tell my mum how I felt, she had her own problems and if I discussed it I soon realised this would be another excuse or reason for her to get drunk.

Every day after school I would hit the swimming pool. I swam at every opportunity I could – school days, tea times, weekends and evenings. I am still to this day not sure if it was because I enjoyed it or if it was because I could not face going home and seeing what state my mother had got herself into from the drinking. Regardless though, at this young time in my life, swimming was my release. It kept me fit, and looking at my skinny body in a swim suit was better than looking at my ugly face and goofy teeth in a mirror. I continued this routine for years. I cannot say it was bad every day at home because it wasn't. We had a lovely big house and I had my own en suite. I loved my room and I loved the house. My mum's husband worked offshore and so when he was away my sister and I felt a little more relaxed in the house. However, whenever he was away my mum would miss him terribly and it seemed to aid her drinking. I didn't really understand it and so I just tried to throw myself into school. I had a small job working as an Avon lady and a paper girl and this kept me out of the house most of the time.

My mum wasn't very strict and so when her husband was away offshore we were left to our own devices. Myself and my sister liked it this way. My pocket money was always spent quickly, going off to the local leisure centre or ice skating and this brought me some really good, happy memories. I was forever going to sleepovers at friends' houses and I loved it, not only because I got away from the troubles of the family home for the night but because going to other people's houses meant I could see how a normal family functioned. I loved it when I got included in family meals at the table at my friends' houses because I always got made a fuss of and I was always allowed to speak. The truth was that at home I was always too scared to speak at the dinner table because I always felt I was being judged by my mum's husband. He had his own daughters and I was nowhere near as good as them in his eyes. Nevertheless, I always had my sister to talk too and we made the best of a bad situation.

We had a small West Highland Terrier dog and when things were strained in the house we always had the excuse of 'walking the dog' to get out for a bit. This continued for years. My little sister seemed to hide away in her room a lot and I guess I didn't blame her. Sometimes I would get frustrated when she wouldn't come out of her room because I needed her to talk to, so that I could also escape the atmosphere that always seemed to loom in our home.

Some days were bearable, but most days I just didn't want to be there at all. It always depended on my mum's husband's mood, if my mum had a hangover and if they had been arguing, as to whether my sister and I were going to be living in silence for the day. The good days were few and far between but – regardless – I loved my mum. On my mum's good days and sober days, I could tell her anything and I felt we were close. We would walk the dog together and go out shopping together, but on her bad days I soon learnt to make myself scarce.

This was just the way it was.

CHAPTER 2: BEING LEFT

In the early spring of the year 2000, my mother and her husband decided to move to Spain.

I was 16 years old but I knew there was no way I was going. I had a turbulent relationship with her husband and I knew I couldn't face seeing my mum kill herself with drink anymore. I loved my mum though and I was devastated.

I will never forget the day she came to my little flat and we said goodbye. My younger sister was going with her. Jenni was four years younger than me and too young to also stay behind, and the day we said goodbye still haunts me. That feeling of 'being left' still affects me in every single way when it comes to being a parent.

When she left with my sister, I sobbed for hours and hours; and it was then that I decided to get drunk. I had never been drunk before, but if it was good enough for my mum, it was good enough for me, right? She seemed to love it so much, there must have been something in it.

I started with a bottle of red Aftershock. This is meant to be a small shot drink, just the odd one from the bottle at a time, but I decided to un-break my heart and just break myself instead; and so I drank the whole entire bottle alone and in one go.

I have no recollection of the next few hours but when I woke up I was in a soaking wet heap laid at the bottom of the stairs and I was covered in my own vomit. I had pissed myself through and through, and I stank.

I felt awful and realised that this had not blocked the pain of my family leaving me at all. Regardless though, it wasn't long before I was going back to the same shop that had sold me that first alcohol under-age and found myself buying more.

As a result, my school days started to reduce even further, from just a few to none at all, and I slowly started hanging out with a bad crowd. I used to love going to school – regardless of feeling the odd one out – but now I found myself working more and more hours to pay the rent and buy food that I just didn't have that much time or energy for school; and when I wasn't working, I just wanted to chill in my flat.

The other kids who once picked on me for looking odd now looked up to me, as I had a cool place to hang out with no adults. I didn't care if they'd bullied me once though, and welcomed them in with open arms – anything to drown out the silence and loneliness of my empty flat.

With that in mind, it wasn't long before my little flat was turned into a teenage lair, where I sat about all day drinking and planning nights out and how to get into clubs whilst being under-age.

But it wasn't long before my manager in JJB Sports and Clark's Shoes started to notice and within the next few weeks I would be sacked from both jobs.

So now I had no money, no way of feeding myself and no way of paying my rent.

However, when my mum rang I would tell her everything was fine.

One teacher at my school tried to help me a number of times; she even bought me food and snuck me bits of money. I was always grateful for the food but I had no idea how to cook so some of the food items she kindly donated to me just went to waste. On numerous occasions I tried to cook pasta in a pan with no water, and I also tried to microwave a meal still completely covered in foil and blew the microwave up. I didn't have the internet and I was too embarrassed to ask someone. I soon realised that trying to eat was more hassle than it was worth, and it wasn't long before I was just living on crisps and pot noodles.

CHAPTER 3:

LET THE STRUGGLES COMMENCE

Not long after losing my jobs, the red letters started to appear. The bills were unpaid and people were looking for their money.

My landlady would often turn up demanding payment and I am not going to lie – I was scared. I was sixteen, I hadn't done this before – paying bills or not paying them, all this was new to me. I used to get to know the days the landlady would be coming round and on those days I avoided my flat and slept rough. I was too scared to go home and – more than anything else – I was ashamed. I had been on my own a matter of months and I had failed.

On 2nd June 2000 I decided to sleep in a park in Culloden. My rent was due on the first of the month and I knew when the landlady realised that yet again it was not in her bank account that she would come looking for me the next day. I was already behind, so she would definitely be coming to see me. Heading for the park, however, would prove to be a near fatal mistake.

I only planned on staying until the early hours of the morning as I knew she would not sit outside my flat all night. I arrived like I had done on a previous occasion, in the late evening. There were still some children on the swings and I could see their parents looking at me with obvious distaste due to the fact I looked like a scruffy teenager just waiting to hang out in a park. They probably thought I just wanted to drink and smoke out of sight from my parents, but this could not be further from the truth. I wanted to run over and tell them I was not bad and I meant no harm, that I just needed this area to sit in for the night. But instead I just sat on the grass and waited until the parents and children headed home; and once they did, I then headed over to a children's pirate ship. It sounds funny but the only reason I picked it is because it offered the most shelter. It had four windows on the bottom floor where you had to climb through a small hole to reach the ground, which would keep me out of the rain. Above me were a pirate's steering wheel and a small seat for sailing the boat.

At around ten o'clock I scurried down to the bottom of the boat, squeezing myself through the small gap to reach the ground floor. It was dirty, there were empty fag packets and booze bottles scattered everywhere, but nevertheless I made the best of what I had.

It was still slightly light, but it was raining. Using the little bit of light left, I scraped some leaves together and made a small pile for my head to rest on. I lay in the dirt patch on the ground, looking out of one of the four circular windows, just staring at the sky. It fascinated me, the colours and how they changed when the sun went down. In some sort of strange way, it seemed to offer me some comfort.

I laid watching and waiting and I did not mean to fall asleep, but I did.

I woke up startled; it was now pitch black in the bottom part of the boat. Without realising, I had curled up in a ball in a drug addict's part of the park; and when they found me asleep, they wanted to know exactly what I was doing there and what I had on me.

I kept telling them I had nothing and that I didn't take drugs but they didn't believe me.

There were two girls and three boys. They looked to be in their early twenties but it was hard to tell because it was dark and there was only a little light coming through the circular windows from the streetlights. I wondered how all five of them got into my small area without me hearing them; but however they'd done it, they were here now and we were all squashed in this claustrophobic area.

They shouted at me to get up and so now with two people behind me and three in front of me, I was told to get on the top part of the boat.

I scurried through the hole back to the top deck like I'd been ordered, and a part of me was relieved because I had felt so panicky in that small confined space in the dark; at least on the top deck I had more of a chance of being able to run away and also I could see more thanks to the streetlights. My relief soon turned to dread though; the girls were drunk and laughing, they started poking me and taunting me.

'You're for it now, bitch,' said one with a sinister giggle, before one of the lads – the main one, the one who seemed to control everything – came right up to me, nose to nose.

'Strip,' he said with an ugly grin. 'Show us what you have or haven't got then.'

I was shaking but I could see a small blade in his hand and so I knew this was not a time to laugh it off or try and run.

With tears running down my cheeks I began to peel off my top. I was already shaking from fright, and the cold rainy air on my skin did nothing to help.

This seemed to make them laugh even more; they took great pleasure in seeing me tremble.

Then I recognized one of them due to the light, and I could see he recognized me too.

'I know you from somewhere,' he said. 'You're that girl that has no parents, aren't you?'

This just made the group erupt with laughter, but the man in front of me seemed to soften a bit and started to ask me more questions as opposed to forcing me to continue with his strip search.

He asked me where I lived and how I managed to go to school if I had no parents. I never answered; I was so scared that I couldn't even look at him, which just seemed to anger him further.

Sniggering, he told me he had seen me in town on a few Saturday nights trying to get into pubs and that if I wanted to act older than I am then I could start right here by showing everyone I wasn't a young innocent girl.

At that, the girls stopped laughing; they could see I had started to cry, and they told him to leave me alone.

But the guy wasn't about to stop. 'Well go on!' he shouted. 'Strip then!'

I was by now already standing in just my jeans and bra. I unfastened my jeans and pulled them off.

'Rob,' the girls shouted 'Rob, you don't have to do this, you can see she's scared.'

This was the first time I'd heard the ring leader's name. I would never forget it.

Once in my underwear he grabbed my arm and I had no idea what was going to happen next; all I knew was that more than anything, I just wanted to go back to my flat and face the music of not paying my rent because that surely had to be a better option than this.

Rob got closer to me and started breathing on my neck. I could smell cigarettes and beer on his breath. It was awful, making me want to vomit.

One of the girls came over then. 'Oi,' she shouted, 'that's enough now, let her go.'

The other two lads were still egging him on. 'Do you two need some privacy?' asked the one I knew.

But then Rob looked me up and down and all of a sudden let go of my arm. 'Look at you,' he spat 'you're not worth catching a disease for.' Then he shoved me away from him, the force so hard I nearly toppled backwards over the top of the boat.

But I managed to stop myself from falling and with that I jumped off the top deck and started running. I didn't even pick up my clothes; I was terrified, humiliated and above all I felt so terribly alone.

I ran back to my flat with no shoes and just wearing my damp soggy underwear; I had been so scared I had left everything else behind.

I arrived back at my flat just after one o'clock in the morning, and I cried until the sun came up.

I lay on my bed the next day, my eyes red raw; I physically couldn't even squeeze out another tear.

Now that the ordeal was over I knew I had to sort my life out; I could no longer live like this.

I never told anyone what had happened, not even my mum when she rang; she would only have worried.

I had my step dad to talk to but he worked offshore and was only home at certain periods. He was very set in his ways and I knew I could not live with him. And to be honest I don't think he would have trusted me in the house whilst he was away with work, and I didn't blame him at all. *I* was starting to not trust me; I simply never knew what was going to happen next in my now so chaotic life.

With no other options left, I decided to call my Dad, who I had met a handful of times since leaving Scarborough as a baby. It was agreed I would move there, and I was relieved to be getting away from my troubles in Inverness but also sad as I had made some lovely friendships. I am still close to Corinne and Victoria now, although at the time I hid how much I was struggling from them because I was so ashamed.

My dad drove all the way from Scarborough to Inverness in a small white van and he picked me and my belongings up. I left that flat in a mess. Unpaid rent and damaged furniture. I ashamedly left it; not my finest moment. For the next few weeks my landlady continued to ring, but I ignored it. She would never find me in Scarborough.

It was a long, long way from Inverness.

The long drive from Inverness to Scarborough was a little awkward. My Dad is not the most talkative man in the world, and aside from anything he was like a stranger to me. I didn't know him and he didn't know me.

When I arrived at his house with his wife and my new baby brother I found it very hard to settle; I felt like I had just invaded someone else's home.

My Dad was never there and was always working and his wife was quite rightly busy with her new-born. She did her best to make me feel welcome but I felt so lost.

Within a month of staying there I decided to join the army. Unsure if I would pass the basic tests, I thought – well, what have I got to lose, I have nothing but a suitcase of belongings and an empty heart so what is the worst that can happen?

Well, I was about to find out.

CHAPTER 4: JOINING THE ARMY

My mother's sister also lived in Scarborough and so I got her to sign my paperwork and come with me for my attestation, my allegiance to the Country.

I was nervous and I found the whole thing quite daunting. In order to be accepted, I needed to travel to Edinburgh to take part in the initial entry tests. This included fitness, team building tests, reactions to discipline, general demeanour and how I conducted myself – not only as an individual but also in a group.

You don't find out until the end of the long weekend if you have passed or not and so the whole time I found myself wondering what I would actually do with myself if I didn't get in. I mean, I had nowhere to go and I knew I did not belong with my Dad; we were two very different people.

Failure was not an option.

On the Sunday after the testing period weekend, I was called into the office by the Army seniors and I nervously stood at attention waiting to be told my fate. I had already told myself I had failed; I mean come on, I seemed to fail at everything. I felt that it was a sheer stroke of luck that I left Inverness with a few GCSE's and decent grades, however right here and right now in this room I knew I was about to be told my failings yet again; and so with the instructor waffling on about how I had conducted myself, I switched off. I started thinking about my next plan of action and how I was going to react when he told me this career was not for me; but then to my amazement, I heard the words, 'Congratulations Victoria, you start in the British Army in September. Now get gone and good luck.'

I had passed my entry tests and fitness tests no problem, and on September 10th 2000 I was on my way to Winchester to start my basic training in the British Army.

It was very scary at first. I was seventeen years old and I had thrown myself into a world I had no idea about and the only reason I found myself there was so I could have a bed to sleep in every night where I didn't feel in the way and also a meal in my belly that I did not have to try and cook myself.

Even the train journey from Scarborough to Winchester was scary; I knew this was my last bit of freedom. I knew in a matter of hours I would be facing sleep deprivation and bollockings. I also knew, on the other hand, that this was what I needed to sort my life out. Discipline, a bed, three cooked meals a day, and a pay packet at the end of it. No matter how scared I felt, I knew I had to do it.

There was no going back.

I arrived at Winchester train station and was politely greeted by an instructor who pointed me to a large coach full of other nervous new recruits just like me. I shuffled onto the bus and plonked myself down. It was silent – nobody was speaking, and so I didn't speak either. The whole journey from the train station to the camp I just looked out the window and thought, 'Goodbye civilian world; I am off to hell voluntarily'.

The first night was fairly relaxed. It was all administration, taking all our details, sussing out who had turned up and who had not, issuing us bed spaces and letting us get settled.

I started to relax a little once in my room with six other girls. They all seemed nice. Most were my age and this helped me realise I was not the only young nervous one. We got to know each other and I soon realised these girls in my room would be my family for the next three months; at last, I was no longer alone.

The next day though, basic training really started.

The relaxed atmosphere had gone and now things were about to get tough, just as I knew they would.

All the shouting and discipline made me very nervous and within my first week of being there I had wet the bed. I had never done this before, but I was utterly humiliated. I was adamant I would not get found out, but I was sharing a room and this was training – of course the beds got stripped off during morning inspection and there was no hiding the stained mattress.

My instructor made sure it was known to everyone on parade that I had ruined a mattress and that I would not only have to pay for it, but I would have to be disciplined for it. I am not sure if my instructor was trying to make an example out of me or if he just saw it all as funny, but it was nevertheless a stupid, nervous mistake.

I had to run around carrying my soggy wet mattress above my head around the parade square for what seemed like hours, although in reality though it was probably much less. But I never wet the bed again; in fact, I never let myself fall into that much of a deep sleep again for the duration of my twelve-week basic training course. It just wasn't worth the risk.

I thoroughly enjoyed basic training once I got into it. I made some great friends and for the first time in many years I felt I had a purpose. There were tough days and days when I just wanted to sleep but all in all this was the Army and it was never going to be easy.

I got along with all the girls in my room and we stuck together as a team and got through it. If one of us had forgotten something on exercise, then we would all muck in and share our own kit. If one of us had a low day we again would all try and cheer that person up. When we were allowed out, after the eighth week in training, we all went together and stuck together. If one of us got too drunk – usually me – then you could guarantee the rest of the girls would ensure that person would get back to camp, and on time.

We were a team.

We always found a way to laugh and have banter in our rooms, even when we were stood ironing our kit past two in the morning and were all absolutely knackered.

There were days when scrubbing the tiles on the bathroom floor with a toothbrush ready for an inspection really broke me, especially when the instructors had looked at the same spot what seemed like ten times and seemed to always find an 'invisible issue'; but on the other hand, looking back now, I think of these memories and smile. It taught me a lot and – suffice to say – my home now is always spotless.

By the end of the course the instructors seemed to like me. They always seemed to laugh at my cheeky sense of humour and my upbeat personality. I tried to remain positive through the whole course, because after all – no matter what was thrown at me – I had a roof over my head and somewhere to eat and sleep.

Here I was achieving something, and so even on my most tired days, I always had this in the back of my mind.

It kept me going and – if I am honest – I think it kept some of the other girls going as well.

In December 2000 after a long twelve weeks, I had completed my Phase One training and I was proud as punch. Now seventeen years old, I felt I had achieved something.

My Dad came to watch me; my Mum did not.

I desperately wanted her to be there. When I marched onto the parade square, my eyes searched for her in the crowd and although I knew she would not be coming over from Spain for the occasion, I really deep down hoped she would. I was smiling on the outside, but inside, part of my heart was still dead. I needed her to see what I had done on my own.

But she wasn't there.

After Christmas 2000 came the start of Phase Two training. This is called your trade training. So basic training is learning your soldier skills but then Phase Two training is learning your job role within the army.

I was looking forward to going back to training, without the army I had nowhere really to go.

In some ways the army had truly saved me.

I had chosen to learn to become an Administrator/Clerk (Combat Human Resource Specialist). I was always good at sorting my own paperwork and admin out, so this appealed to me. I also got an 'A' in Secretarial Studies, so I thought this career trade choice suited me well.

There were some girls from basic training starting Phase Two training with me and I was looking forward to seeing them after that break away from each other. I was not as nervous turning up for Phase Two as I was for Phase One. I had heard on the grapevine it was not as strict and you got more downtime. Not so many inspections, not so many fitness tests, and not as much sleeping outside under a poncho. All this was like music to my ears.

So January 2001 came, and I cracked on. I had already done the hardest part, and by now I started to believe in myself.

I knew I could do this.

The best part of my Phase Two training was passing my driving test first time. I felt so proud. Seventeen years old and I had joined the army, passed my training with no issues, and had now learnt to drive. Affording a car would be another story, but none the less, I could drive.

For my twelve-week Phase Two training, my partying ways started to creep up on me and I think I spent most of the course hiding the effects of drunken nights out. I always seemed to pass my fitness tests and my classroom tests but I actually to this day have no idea how, I always seemed to be masking the effects of the previous nights out in the bar.

There was many a time I would be stood on the parade square very hungover. I had a cheeky bubbly personality and the instructors always asked me even when I was sober if I was in fact drunk! I was so bubbly in character that I guess they just thought, well you would have to be drunk to have the balls to answer back the way she does and in such a happy smiley way. They could just never tell the difference.

In some ways I quite liked the banter and keeping everyone guessing.

The majority of Phase Two training was spent in classrooms, learning the basic clerking skills that would set me up in my unit once I finished training. It was twelve weeks of classroom lessons followed by an end of week test on a Friday prior to weekend dispersal. In Phase Two, your weekends are more or less your own except for the odd one or two when you are on exercise, sleeping in a field.

There was definitely a lot less running around compared to Phase One and I was happy. Some of the tests on a Friday were hard but to be fair if you failed the instructor would then sit down with you and show you where you went wrong and then let you re-sit it.

By March 2001 my time in training had come to an end and so loomed my first ever post to a unit.

There were some girls who I had been in Phase One training with and also Phase Two training and the thought of being separated from them after near seven months of constantly living together made me feel very sad. They were like my sisters.

Part of me wanted to go back to September 2000 and do it all again as this seemed easier than saying goodbye.

However, I knew this was not feasible and so the time had come too say goodbye for now.

The thought of arriving at my new unit made me really bloody nervous. I hadn't actually listened most of the time during the past twelve weeks in the class and I had no idea what I was doing or what to expect. My partying days were about to end and shit seemed to get real! In a few months I would be eighteen and I knew what that meant – I could be deployed overseas.

Shit, I could be off to a war torn country to be an actual soldier.

Holy crap, I was not ready for this; I'd just joined the army for somewhere to live and a bit of money. The thought of actually going to war had not once entered my head until now.

Once again I started to question if I had it in me to stick it out but no matter what, I knew I had no choice; once again, going back was not an option.

I had nothing to go back too.

CHAPTER 5: ARRIVING AT MY UNIT

My first posting was to an Infantry Battalion based in Salisbury.

I arrived at the end of March and most of the unit had already been stood down for Easter Leave so camp was fairly quiet. I settled okay but I was uneasy. There were very few girls in the female block. This was not like training where we all had shared a room and there was always someone to talk too, this was a working unit and most trained soldiers had family homes they lived in or went to after work.

I think I was 1 of 3 females who lived in the block in my own room. I felt very alone and isolated and I hated it. I made a few friends but I certainly did not enjoy the structure of this camp or this unit.

My first day everyone stared at me. I knew that would happen though because I was in a male dominant unit. A new female in this type of environment would always cause this type of reaction. Like throwing a lamb to the slaughter. I tried to ignore comments in the cook house, again just like school, people would stare at me. My scrawny skinny body in an army uniform. I just looked ridiculous. The uniform hung off me and without make up I looked like something from a horror movie but still I plodded on.

I was initially sent to work in the Headquarters of camp as one of the Officer's assistant. There was a nice civilian lady that I worked with and when I got stuck or couldn't find the answer to something, then she would help me.

The main administration office was at the other end of the building and to be honest despite being in an administrative role I avoided this main office like the plague. It scared me. There were always high ranks in there asking questions or putting me on the spot and I hated it. It made me nervous. I wasn't ready for constant questions on pay queries or the rules and regulations, not so soon out of training anyways so for most of the time I hid in the small office with this one lady and tried to keep my head down.

I had made friends with the man who worked in the mail room. Whenever I needed a break from the office I would go and chat to him, this broke up my day a little. Regimental Routine was not like training at all and although it was easier than training I found myself wishing to be back in that environment where I felt not so alone and in the exact same boat as all the other recruits. Here I just felt isolated. I tried my hardest to make friends but all the other clerks were a lot older than me and all had husbands/wives/family and so on, none of which I had and so conversation always seemed to dry up.

It was not long before a work colleague in the office introduced me to a soldier called John. Little did I know then that this man would remain in my life forever and to this very day is one of my best friends. I think we were introduced because John was the one who all the junior soldiers went to if they needed advice or their feet taping up before a Bergen run. I forever had bad blistered feet after the long gruelling training runs and so I was sent down to the male block for John to look at my feet. He had been in the army years and seemed to know exactly what he was doing.

When I arrived at his room he had a queue of soldiers at his door, it was his section wanting help with kit packing ready for an exercise. However, he stopped everything and spoke to me. I can't really remember what we spoke about but I do remember his crazy dancing and I thought he seemed funny.

I wasn't at the Regiment long before we exchanged numbers and we soon started dating. I would tell John daily how much I didn't think the army life was for me anymore and that I disliked the unit. I felt way out of my depth. By June 2001 John was deployed to Sierra Leone. I stayed behind as I was under 18. He was there for 6 months training the African soldiers on how to defend themselves and basic soldiering skills. Something he really enjoyed. He was in his element.

In August 2001 I was drunkenly assaulted by a small group of other soldiers on camp.

With all other females in my room deployed to Sierra Leone (they were over 18), this just left me alone in the accommodation block and so after a small gathering where soldiers got together and had a drink in the main communal part of the building things got out of hand and I found myself in a very vulnerable position.

At the time I was the only female there (I had made friends with a female chef but she worked some crazy hours and she was never there when I was in my room) and had I thought about it before, drinking with other young lads alone was not one of my best ideas. I had a small dog that I was looking after for company and after the attack I cried for ages, cuddling this dog. It took me ages to process what had happened and when the lad I had made friends with in the mail room came to see me and realised what state I was left in he reported it to the guard room.

Before I knew it there was police knocking on my door and I was whisked down to the civilian police station to give a statement. I was thoroughly distressed and upset and I could not believe all this was happening. I never wanted to be a burden on my new unit and by now that is what I felt I was. The group in question were also interviewed but by now they had already been told they had been reported and they all had word perfect stories to back them up. It was my word against theirs. Once again I was a lone warrior. I hated it. I hated being on my own.

The police questioning felt more like an interrogation and I am sure to this day they thought I was making it up. My Mum was called in Spain but again I asked her not to come. It was another let down on my part, I felt.

After a few weeks of constant questioning and missing work, I'd had enough.

John was flown back from Sierra Leone for a short time to give me some support (something the army did not have to do as we had not been a couple that long and we were not married) and it was at this point I decided to hang up my army boots.

By September 2001 I decided to exercise my right to be discharged prior to my eighteenth birthday. However, actually getting out would take a few weeks whilst I waited for the paperwork to be completed so this meant I was on solid guard duty from now until I was out.

On September the eleventh, when the terrorist attacks hit America, I was sat on guard duty watching the news unfold on the TV. I was absolutely terrified; I went to my bunk bed in the guard room and cried my eyes out.

The other soldiers on duty were laughing at me but I didn't care, I couldn't stop. I don't know if I was crying because of what happened or because I was relieved that I was too young (still under 18) to have to go anywhere near there to help. Selfish I know, but I knew I would be useless.

After the incident on camp I was a nervous wreck. I wasn't ready for anything remotely war like. Let alone helping with terrorist attacks. I couldn't believe what I was seeing on the TV and I just knew getting out the army at that time for me was the right thing to do.

Right then though at that precise moment in that guard room I actually felt so alone and so scared. I really thought, that's it, they are coming here next and I am stuck in this room with people I don't even know the name of.

My thoughts then turned to John, what if they sent him straight out there to help. What if he didn't come back from Sierra Leone? I would be stuck here alone with no one. I was really angry at myself for having all these selfish thoughts. Hundreds of people dead and here I am having a panic.

I didn't know it at the time but this was my first ever panic attack. I had cried so much I was hyper ventilating. I could not put my thoughts into any logical reason. I could not see past the black clouds. I could not hear my fellow comrades talking to me. I do not remember anything for the rest of that night. I full blown panicked. RIP to all the men, woman and children who tragically lost their lives that day. Unbelievable evil.

John did return to Sierra Leone to continue with the work he was doing out there, he always remained professional and would not leave a job half finished. I commend him for that. I am now glad he went back out there and finished what he started because they needed him far more than I did; this was just another Vikki blip in the grand scheme of things.

CHAPTER 6: LEAVING THE ARMY

On 15th November 2001 I was discharged from the British Army with Exemplary Service. I had completed 1 year and 56 days' service. Hardly anything in the real world but for me it was enough to start me off in life. I had gained a bit of experience, I had made some money and now I could drive.

I was now eighteen and I decided to head back to Scarborough whilst I waited for John to get out the Army. He had signed off too but because he had completed near twelve years he had to give a year's notice to be discharged.

I had got from the Army for now what I needed; but this would not be the only time I would use the army to help me get back on track.

I initially moved back in with my Dad but again we were like strangers and it didn't work out.

In March 2002 I realised I was expecting. John was over the moon but very worried as we had nowhere stable to live and he had also signed off from the army and so he would soon be jobless. He had to carry out the rest of his service in Cyprus (where the Regiment were currently working) and so with the fact things were strained with me and my Dad I decided to fly out there and stay with him as a civilian not a soldier just for a whilst.

I lived in a private rented small flat which cost £300 per month. I was just willing the time along until he got out, I was very alone.

It was in Cyprus where we married. On 27th April 2002 we got married in a Church overlooking the sea. We did not have a lot of money but we made the best of it.

Again my Mum did not come but my Dad did. He walked me down the aisle. It was here I started to get to know my father. It was a lovely day and although I had no real close friends nor family there I remember this as a very happy occasion.

I very much missed my mum and my sister but it just wasn't meant to be. John's parents made me feel very welcome into the family and for the first time since my mum and my sister left I felt happy.

After a few months living in Cyprus I then went back to Scarborough at my auntie's. She had a room in her house. It wasn't the best house but I was grateful for the room and the fact she had taken me in. In September 2002 John was discharged and he came to live with me in the tiny room in my auntie's house.

We put a Moses basket in there and a small baby changing table and we had a kettle and a TV and a small fridge and a few personal belongings and that was it. That is how we lived. John started training for the police around a month before my due date so it meant I was very much again on my own in this little room waiting to drop. I was worried if John would get back from training on time for when I went into labour. However, I was overdue and so I was scheduled in for an induction and so this meant I had an exact date I needed John to be there and not in Police training.

My mum travelled to Scarborough to visit me and to be there for the birth of my first born. It was hard because we were both stuck in this small cramped room waiting for the delivery day and I knew she hated the conditions and just wanted to return home. I was grateful for her coming though but embarrassed that I had nothing to show her but this little room. I spent my days walking along the beach to pass the time. I had no money for nice lunches or even an ice cream but with fresh air in my lungs I remained optimistic.

CHAPTER 7: NEW ARRIVAL

On 16th October 2002, Abigail Jade was born. I wasn't alone any more. I was now a mother. I was now responsible for another life.

I was over the moon but at the same time extremely worried. We had no stable home, we had debt and John was going to be in training ages meaning I was on my own with nothing. I knew he had to be away because if he didn't pass his training then we would be jobless altogether.

The house I was staying in was filthy. No fault of my aunty, she had her own problems after divorce and was working all the hours God sent to keep on her feet.

The couple in the room next to me smoked drugs and it stank. The one toilet was a few floors down and it was freezing and I was scared leaving Abi alone in the room whilst I went to the toilet so most of the time I traipsed her with me.

I could be in there for hours at a time, I had no money for baby milk leaving me no option but to breastfeed and this left me with horrendous constipation. I didn't drink enough fluids because I could not afford fancy juices and I hated coming out of my room to go to the kitchen for a glass of water for fear of bumping into the endless people that seemed to tread through the house.

I also couldn't rely on the kettle for baby milk because the electricity meter was forever running out. Sometimes it would be a day or so before anyone would put money in the meter. I knew I couldn't afford to top it up, I was barely just surviving myself. For days on end I would sit in my dirty, damp, cold room sometimes in the dark with nothing to look at but my beautiful baby.

She is what kept me alive. I certainly couldn't end it now. There was no way I was leaving my baby in this.

Right there in my arms was the strength I needed to get through this.

On one of the rare occasions that John managed to come home we decided to go to his parents' house for the weekend.

However, on my return back to my room in that house, where all the belongings I had in the world were, I soon discovered I had been burgled. My few things were now even fewer.

My TV was gone, my DVDs had been taken and Abi's Moses basket was saturated in piss. Someone obviously thought the trek in the dark to the toilet was too much to bear and they peed in her baby bed. I was devastated. I had nothing left. I clung to my baby and sobbed for hours.

A few months after that, with a lot of help from Johns parents we bought our own house. We knew John was going to be a Police Officer in Leeds West Yorkshire but I did not want to live in such a big city and so we bought a house in Wakefield West Yorkshire, just a few miles away.

By May 2003 we were home owners. We moved into our own house and I was overjoyed. We had no furniture and no money for furniture but I was just happy to be in our own home.

We got into debt from there rather quickly what with buying things for the house and just living outside of our means. So very soon our relationship started to deteriorate. Little did we know our house was also deteriorating, it was crumbling from beneath us and so we put it on the market and it sold. We broke even.

CHAPTER 8: SEPARATION

It wasn't long after that, that we separated. In 2005 I can safely say the stresses of money or lack of it and my up and down moods lead to a breakdown of our marriage.

We had been living like brother and sister for a whilst and so I had started to go out more and more. Part of me also resented the fact he had got his career whilst I had the initial struggles in a hell whole house looking after our baby alone (I do know it wasn't his fault though, it's just how I felt at the time).

I felt like I had gone through too much stress and worry young and now was my time to live through my youth.

During this time I met someone else. I am not proud of myself in any way for breaking up the family but regardless if I had met someone else or not our marriage would have still been over.

It was also the first real time I had started to make real life adult friends. Laugh as you will but I had never been settled long enough to make friends and since my basic training army days, I did not really have any girlfriends I could go out and hang around with. I spent all my time in Scarborough more or less alone.

However, since moving to Wakefield I had got a small part time job at a catalogue firm and it was here I made my first real friends since school. I couldn't wait to start going out more after being cooped up in a room for so long with a baby and no money at all.

Working part time at the catalogue firm and I soon met my best friends. I firmly believe everything happens in your life for a reason and I really believe the reason I took that shitty job was so I could meet Kati and Clare (more on these ladies later).

So now it was time for John to leave, I did feel a little sad but I knew it was for the best, we had grown apart. John bought a house not so far away (so we could share childcare when he was not working) and in time I also moved into a rented two-bedroom property with this new person I was now dating.

Unknown to me at the time moving in with this new man was to be one of my biggest mistakes in my life. He was by no means at all bad, in fact he was and still is a lovely young man but this new relationship did not last long. He was younger than me and we did nothing but argue.

I was so scared of being alone that it drove him away. It was over a year and half of us being on and off but in spring 2007 we separated for good, the whole experience left me major low. Once again I was on my own.

My biggest fear more than anything in the world. Even now the thought of it makes me have endless panic attacks. I should have gone for help. I should have seen a doctor. Hindsight is a wonderful thing but at the time I felt like John still hated me for separating and was just waiting for my first fall before he could convince the courts Abi was to live with him for good (he wasn't but that's how I thought).

So in my head what use was going to the doctor and documenting the fact I was suffering with low moods and panic attacks? To me that would be the worst move I could make because then John would have it all in black and white that I was in fact mentally ill. What court in the land would let a five-year-old stay with a mentally ill parent on their own in a rented house over living in a bought property with a police officer parent?

That is honestly what I thought and so it was in summer 2007 I had my first experience with drugs.

I was 24 years old and had always been proud I had never even smoked a cigarette, but now here I was at rock bottom.

CHAPTER 9: <u>THE DRUGS DON'T WORK</u>

Abi started going to her dad's most weekends and this left me alone. Most single parents love alone time but not me. I hated (and still do hate) the silence, I also felt lost. If I wasn't looking after my daughter, then I didn't really have a purpose.

I was already feeling low so sitting in my empty flat without Abi all weekend would not help me.

In order to stop sitting in and feeling sorry for myself and reliving past experiences over and over in my head I decided to go out and socialise and try bring some fun times to my life. I mean, yes I was a parent, but I was allowed to live too, right? I would much rather have had Abi with me every single weekend but these were just selfish thoughts. Her dad was her parent too and I could not cling on to her for my own sole purpose of keeping me happy and busy.

So every single weekend when she went to her dads I hit town with friends to fulfil the feeling of not being alone. In order to take my mind off my lows, my failures and my struggles, I drank heavily. A few months of always going out and before I knew it I was hanging out with the popular people. The people that could walk past bouncers and not pay into clubs, the kind of people that were allowed to stay in for lock-ins and after-hours drinks, the people that seemed to get lots of attention up town. The kind of people who others would always buy them a drink if you see them.

I must admit that I loved it. I had never been popular and so I just wanted desperately to be part of this group. I really wanted to fit in and I knew that meant doing whatever it takes.

I was always a nervous person; my only way to conquer my nerves was to drink. It gave me an unfounded confidence. I could easy talk in public or be brave enough to strike up a conversation if I had had a drink in me.

Trouble was, I was going out with these people more and more and so I was drinking more and more. I also couldn't afford all these nights out but – regardless – I always found the money from somewhere. Doorstep loans, payday loans, selling stuff I no longer needed. I even sold my £2,000 engagement ring from John for just over £400, just to fund a couple more nights out – not one of my proudest moments.

It wasn't long before my Thursday nights to Monday mornings of pure partying and drinking binges would take its toll and I soon found myself out of work. It was then that I realised I was spending hundreds of pounds on drink and I was skint, I had nothing. I had hit an all-time low.

That's when someone mentioned trying cocaine. They told me at £30 a bag it would be cheaper than buying rounds of drinks all night and it had the same effect and that I would instantly feel happy.

I was naïve and I listened intently, thinking *wow, I would love to feel happy again* and so I watched this person roll a bank note and make small white powdery lines which was cut up into rows with a bank card.

They had sniffed two lines using the rolled up note and then said, 'Here you go Vikki, try it, be happy.'

With a room full of people all staring at me I felt I should and before I knew it I had snorted two lines of cocaine.

I looked up and laughed it off but inside I was dying. This didn't make me feel happy at all, in fact right at that precise moment I felt utter shame. I had just really let myself down. I had made it to 26 without even smoking and now I was shoving Class A drugs up my nose to try and impress other people and outwit my lows just so I could just fit in.

After snorting the drug, I initially had no idea what all the fuss was about, all it did was make my nose tingle. What a complete waste, I thought!

However, ten minutes on and I soon felt giggly and confident like I could just strike up a conversation without fear. I purchased my first ever bag of cocaine and stuffed it into the bottom of my handbag ready to take when out.

I could hear myself talking but it was just nonsense and trivia coming out of my mouth. If I was watching me, I would have laughed at myself because this person seemed an utter joke.

I downed the rest of my wine that I was drinking at this small house party and headed out the door to town high on drugs and what I thought was 'worry and care free'.

That person was right, I did feel happy.

The first few nights of taking the drug I felt really happy, confident and empowered, like nothing or no one could bring me down. I always went to the toilets and sat in there and had a line or two with people who I thought were my friends.

At first I couldn't believe how many girls were doing this, I could hear other groups of girls all piled into one toilet cubicle and also all doing the exact same thing I was doing. It soon became clear to me that it was very much the done thing and it seemed nearly everyone was at it. Even the door staff knew what was going on and they all seemed to be turning a blind eye to it.

I had never noticed before on prior nights out and I soon realised how naïve and oblivious I was to it all. I loved how the drug made me feel and it wasn't long until one bag of cocaine wasn't enough. I needed more.

At £30 a bag (a gram) though and not working, I soon realised it was called 'the rich man's drug' for a reason. In 2007 I went onto benefits for the first ever time (and I am ashamed to say it) and I used some of this money to pay for my drugs.

I was one of *those* people. People I now see as thieves and benefit players, taking out of the Government's purse to fund their habits. I was not claiming a lot, I think £45 a week. I spent £15 a week on food and £30 a week on drugs. Even writing this on paper, I could easily cry. It was such a shallow thing to do and I am not proud, I am very ashamed of myself for this fact. However, the £30.00 a week was not enough for me because with taking the drugs and receiving the highs also came the lows.

This was the worst part. I was already depressed, so having cocaine 'come downs' on top of depression was like hell on earth. I can honestly say I never, ever want to go through anything like that again. In order to try and outwit the low points I would get my hands on more.

Soon I knew the dealers in the local area and I could easily get cocaine on credit. I would take the drug but still owe the money – a very dangerous game.

My weekdays now seemed to all consolidate into one long week. With taking drugs I was never really that tired and so shutting my brain down on a night time to sleep was non-existent. My long weekends of partying, I hardly slept. I could go Thursday night to Monday morning without even returning home (when Abi was at her dad's), and if people got fed up in town I would venture off to one of the many house parties that seemed to be happening – again a drug filled venue of just sitting around listening to music, drinking and taking drugs.

When the weekend was over I tried to function to the best of my ability in order to carry on the pretence that I was a fully-functioning adult with a child.

I would walk Abi to school, come home to my empty, quiet, lacklustre home and within ten minutes find myself bored – and so I would snort some cocaine in order to feel happy for an hour or so. This helped pass the time until Abi was home.

I was now taking the drug through the week. I always made it to school and was never late for her but by now my existence seemed to be solely chemical-related. With the drug I didn't feel bored or alone or sad and without it, well – I just felt (at that time) that I had nothing and that my world was going to end. I was absorbed into a world that was false.

I was only happy when I had chemicals swirling through my system, and I didn't want it to end.

CHAPTER 10:

SPIRALLING OUT OF CONTROL

On many occasions whilst out and high – or 'happy' as I liked to call it – I would order more. Sometimes I couldn't even remember how much I ordered and most of the time I didn't want to know.

Whilst high on drugs and out with no money, I would mine-sweep drinks; this is where if you see a glass with drink in it on the side of a bar somewhere you just take it and drink it. Therefore, it looks like you have a drink and also it saved me buying one.

Again, another risky game. You never knew what you were getting and the drinks could have been laced with anything. This was so true one night because after taking three bags of cocaine and mine-sweeping all evening, I started to feel really sick.

This wasn't a happy feeling, this was a scary feeling, my legs had gone to jelly and I had sweat droplets running down my head. My heart was racing and I felt really dizzy. I had no idea where I was and the bright lights of the club made me feel like a startled deer in the headlights.

The fast music beats of the club seemed to be in time with my now rapid heartbeat and I tried desperately to find somewhere to sit down; but amongst all the crowds and clubbers I was not getting anywhere fast. The room seemed to consume me and I was now seeing white sparkly stars. I thought I was dying.

In fact, I hoped I was dying. It had to be less scary than this.

That was my last thought before I collapsed.

I had lost my friends somewhere in the club, so when I fainted and hit the floor I was alone. The bouncers must have thrown me out but rather than get me help they had thrown me out the fire exit around the back entrance and when I woke up the next morning I was laid in a skip in just my underwear at the bottom of the club's fire exit stairwell.

I was covered in my own vomit. It was in my hair, I had bits of sick stuck to my face, my eyes felt puffy and swollen and I was freezing.

I looked around and could not see anyone. I had no idea what day it was, nor the time for that matter and I wondered how long I had been out cold for and why my friends weren't looking for me.

I soon realised my bag was gone. I had no phone or money and I knew John would have been ringing me so I could speak to Abi.

I started to panic, I had no idea what had happened. I was violently sick. I could see my clothes at the bottom of the fire exit stairs and so I scurried out and quickly put them on. I then walked home absolutely freezing and with no shoes, and once there I cried for hours, if not days.

I sat in the bath desperately trying to recall what had happened but there was nothing. I have no idea what occurred during the twelve or more hours that I was out cold.

After a few hours, I scavenged the house for some change so I could go and telephone John and check on Abi. When I spoke to him he told me he had been trying to ring me since Friday. I knew Friday night was the night I went out so I merely asked him what day it was now? He told me it was Sunday.

I had been in there from the early hours of Saturday morning right through to Sunday lunchtime. No wonder I was still struggling to get my body temperature regulated. I couldn't believe what a mess I had got myself in. I told him that I thought I had been spiked and I had no money and no phone, but I don't think he believed me.

He did come down to the house though and tried to help. He advised me to stay in for a while and drink plenty of fluids. I knew on Monday I could sort out my bank cards that was no missing. For now though, I just needed to be thankful I was here and more importantly than that so was Abi.

She was now home and I had a duty to look after her. This was not the time to dwell on the mess I had put myself in.

Now, you might think that this whole experience would have made me want to change my ways and never touch drugs again; but in fact it did the complete opposite.

After a week of thinking about the whole sordid experience, I was now so low that all I could think about was drugs to fix my crappy memories. However, I did stay in for a few days and just cried and I did think to myself that I should really now seek help, but again I was too scared.

Instead, I contacted all my friends to find out who was out the following weekend and to make plans. With the weekend plans I made, I knew I only had a few days in my hell-hole existence to get through until I had my happy feelings back.

I continued mummy duties as best as I could but it was always a struggle. Even on food shopping I had sunk to an all-time low. I was now stealing. Not only was I a drug addict, but I was now a thief. I always dressed smartly and so I don't think the supermarket staff suspected a thing, so I got away with it.

I didn't steal for fun, I didn't steal to make money from it, I stole to survive. I always paid for most items at the checkout but the more expensive items that I couldn't afford were stolen.

This is how I did it. When I needed new make-up or toiletries I would make holes in the cereal boxes, just enough to push things through but not big enough to alarm the checkout operators. I also switched labels. So a ten-pound joint of meat would now have a one-pound barcode on it. I would always smash an egg inside the egg box and so when I got to the checkout and it was leaking, I knew the staff would offer to switch it – but instead I would say I'd just take it as it is, knowing full well they would discount it or give it to me for free.

When it was people's birthdays I would always pick a nice £3 to £4 birthday card and put it inside a 60p magazine. Remembering family and friends' birthdays was always important to me, I needed to try and keep up the pretence that everything was okay.

I kept up this sordid thieving routine for a few months but I hated myself for it. Every time I went to the checkout, my heart would be beating so fast I was sure I was about to alarm someone. But I never did.

Sometimes I wished I *would* get caught, because it might have given me the kick up the arse I needed sooner.

Supermarket trips for Abi was great though. I always let her eat as much as she could in the trolley on the way around the aisles, ensuring she was full and hiding the wrappers in various places around the stalls. She loved it. Entirely wrong but it was like a mini-Christmas to her as our house always just had the basic food supplies in it.

It should never have been that way – not in a million years – but because of my own stupidity, it was now how I lived.

CHAPTER 11:

THE WORST EXPERIENCE OF MY LIFE

Christmas 2007 was soon here and with that so was the thought of money and providing presents for Abi. No easy task with no money and a lot of debt and a spiralling addiction; however, I knew I would somehow manage it.

By now depression had really taken a hold of me and I was struggling to even get dressed on a morning. I tried so hard to hide my tears from my five-year-old but it wasn't easy. Now I was so fixated on my weekend highs it was the only thing getting me through my dire straits week. I had a beautiful daughter but at that time I was blinded by my own stupidity and disgust in myself that I needed my weekly fixes to function or give me an aim.

I had no idea how much I owed my drug dealer and most of the time I tried to avoid that person because I didn't want to know. I then started getting credit with another drug dealer. By now I had been on drugs for four months but that was all it took to take hold.

I was sick of my sorrowful existence.

I was sick of living.

I was just sick.

Christmas Eve and Christmas Day 2007 were – to this day – the worst point in my life. Over and above everything I have never, ever been as low as I was that day.

Christmas Eve was the day I had had enough.

I finally tried to end it.

How the hell had I gotten so bad? I can only describe it as living in the dark. I knew what I was doing was wrong but I just could not stop. I was addicted to that tiny feeling of happiness that I got from drugs even if it did only last a few minutes. The lows that followed were immense, I could not cope, I was weak. I had had enough of trying to be strong. I knew I needed help but was so scared of losing Abi and feeling the pain that goes with it that I decided losing me instead would be the easier option, and so I wrote my letter to Abigail prior to trying to not live in the dark anymore.

It read:

My darling Abigail, I have failed you. I have let you down more than words can say. I know this. Don't think I haven't tried because I have. Don't think I don't love you because there are not enough words in the English language to describe the love I have for you. From the minute you arrived I have loved you with every inch of my heart. You deserve the world and I cannot give you it. God knows I have tried. You deserve so much better than my failings, you deserve so much more than a mother battling demons and neglecting you. You deserve a better mummy and the only way you can get that is if I am no longer around to selfishly keep you with me. Your daddy will take brilliant care of you. Don't cry for me my darling because I am always near you, I will always be watching over you and protecting you from afar where I cannot cause any more damage. Your daddy will be here when you wake up and I want you to open your presents and be happy that you are free of the burden of me. I want you to remember the happy times we had and remember the days we laughed and did not cry. Whenever you feel sad or are scared please look up at the Sky and I will be the sun in your dark days and the stars in your night time. I will shine brightly for you forever. I love you, I always have and I always will. You are my beautiful Abigail and you are my world. Merry Christmas Darling, Love Mum xxxx

I pushed the letter under her pillow and kissed her on the head, I watched her sleeping for a few minutes but I couldn't stay too long because the pain was killing me.

I needed it over.

With that, I closed her bedroom door and headed down the stairs.

CHAPTER 12: READY TO DIE

I had the family photograph in my left hand and the needle in my right.

I pierced into the vein on my left arm, feeling the sting, and I was about to press down hard to inject the heroin that would seal my fate, when it happened.

The miracle.

Just as I was about to throw my life away, I heard the living room door open.

And in the door way stood Abigail.

She never wakes up at night time, I remember thinking. Why the hell had she got up now?

She stood there rubbing her eyes. 'Mummy,' she said softly, 'has Santa been?'

With that, I pulled the needle out of my arm and ran over to her.

I scooped her up and cuddled her like I have never cuddled anyone before.

My daughter had just saved my life.

Ten minutes later and I would have been well on my way to death.

I made us a hot drink and went back up to bed. I cuddled her for hours, until she was settled and had gone back to sleep. With that, I got up wrapped her presents up properly – I had just left them wrapped in carrier bags prior to this – and laid them out nicely for her for morning.

Then I flushed my drugs down the toilet and disposed of the needle.

Through that entire ordeal it hadn't even crossed my mind once that had I gone through with this suicide, that my little girl's Christmas would have been ruined forever.

Every Christmas from there on in could have been spent with the memory of finding her mother dead in a slumped heap on Christmas morning.

I had been so selfish. What was I thinking?

Still, I was so very sad.

Depression was by no way finished with me yet.

On a side note, this whole experience is when I firmly started to believe in Spiritualism.

I now believe I was saved for a reason.

I believe someone up there was looking out for me, and my daughter that night for some reason got up to save me.

I now will always believe in spiritualist guidance.

Christmas morning came and I watched Abi open her presents.

I painted a smile on my face and tried to be OK for her sake. She was delighted with her gifts.

I made us breakfast and it wasn't long until John had turned up. After all, I did tell him to come early Christmas morning; I was expecting me not to be there any longer.

However, there I was and it was Christmas – come on Vikki, its bloody Christmas! Nope, I couldn't even raise a smile. And Christmas Day was now going to drag even more with Abi away for even longer.

As soon as Abi was gone I took down the Christmas tree. I couldn't stand the sight of it. I threw the turkey away, I took down all the Christmas cards, and I put all Abi's gifts into her bedroom and closed the door.

I also took down all the mirrors in the house; all I could see when I looked in them was a disgusting thief and a failure staring back at me, and so the mirrors had to go.

I mean, I couldn't even kill myself correctly.

What an idiot, I thought.

I started boxing up all my personal belongings, the things that really mattered to me like letters from my mum when she lived in Spain, letters from John when we were very much in love and he was working in Sierra Leone, family photos, bits of jewellery, my necklace my grandma and granddad had sent to me on my 18th birthday in 2001, my happy family photos from when I was a child and then lastly I collected my goodbye letter I had written to Abi only a few hours earlier.

I put all the things together and sealed it in a box. I knew I was going to die soon – or hoped I would – and I wanted all these things kept somewhere safe and together for Abi for when she was older.

Once I had done all that I turned my TV around so it faced the wall. There was no way I was switching that thing on, on Christmas Day, just to be reminded of how happy the outside world was when I was dying inside.

I went to bed and cried. My little shit French bed on the floor was now my haven for the next few days. I remained there, ignoring my phone and any acknowledgement to the world. My friends would text and ask me what my plans were for New Year's but I couldn't even find it in myself to reply.

New Year!!! I didn't want New Year to come, and why would I? Just so I could struggle through another year merely existing and not actually living?

But now it was going to be far worse.

I owed thousands.

I was finished, physically and mentally.

CHAPTER 13: NEW YEAR'S EVE 2007

New Year's was here, and what did I do?

I went out!

I knew deep down it was the wrong thing to do but I had nothing at this shit-hole house to stay in for.

The drug dealer I owed lots of money to caught up with me and gave me a warning about paying some of it back. He was angry and shouting and I knew I had pissed him off with all my false promises of repayments. I promised once again that I would have his money soon but – quite rightly – he did not believe me. He told me it was all too little, too late – and due to always letting him down, I was now going to have to help him out.

He needed someone to help with drug deals and so for now I was going to be their puppet.

I was gutted. I knew I had no choice because I had got myself in this mess and I knew I owed him.

I was now a drug mule.

Drugs in Wakefield had got so bad that police officers stood on the streets with sniffer dogs. This made dealing hard; it was hard to carry drugs without the police dogs smelling them out.

I was given twelve bags of cocaine to carry into a club, so that once inside they could be dealt. Not by me, but by the dealer.

I was now getting used as a carrier, but I couldn't argue. I owed money, I could hardly say no. In return for carrying some drugs here, there and everywhere it was agreed that some of my debt would be written off.

Sometimes, if I was lucky, I would also get a free bag of coke for my troubles. This was like the jackpot to me at the time.

So here I was on New Year's Eve going into 2008, now effectively an assistant dealer. I was carrying drugs for horrible people. I never really thought of the repercussions, I just knew if I didn't do it I would be beaten up for sure, if not worse.

If I am honest, I was a bit scared but I tried not to think about what I was actually doing. I was so ashamed of myself. I couldn't believe I had let myself sink this low. I wanted to go to the police station and hand myself in and ask for help but the fear of losing Abi always outweighed doing the right thing. Why would the police help me when I had got myself into this situation?

I didn't want to tell my family or friends because once again I was failing at life and they would only be even more ashamed of me.

I was in this for the long haul, and so with no choice I reluctantly stuffed the drugs into every nook and cranny of the under garments on my body.

My first night of doing this I felt physically sick. I was scum. I was now helping criminals sell their loot in order to pay off some of my disgusting blood money. I call it blood money because someone, somewhere, probably got made to get the coke I had previously taken and had also suffered at the hands of these criminals.

I was now starting to see the bigger picture, and it made me scared.

Carrying drugs is a very scary thing to do. I had to time everything to a tee; for instance, walking through club doors in a large group so I did not attract attention to myself, I wore big pants and even started putting the drugs in the lining of scented sanitary towels in order for the smell to be less from sniffer dogs.

Had I at any time been caught, I knew I would be facing jail for a very long time. Ironically I lived right next to Wakefield Prison; and I always thought that one day I was going to be in it. It was a terrifying thought, but nevertheless I continued with carrying the drugs; I was more scared of what would have happened if I didn't do what was asked of me.

Most days I wished I could just disappear. I wanted the ground to open up and swallow me.

My first drop to the dealers was immense. I was sweating and I was sure I was about to be caught. The paranoia you suffer when carrying drugs is unreal. You think everyone but everyone is looking at you because they know. You think the door staff are going to search you, you think the police are following you, you think people all around you know what you are doing, you think you are going to get caught at any minute and for the entire duration my heart has never beat so fast.

I hated it. This was not me at all but for now, circumstances said otherwise.

I located the drug dealer in the club and he was surrounded by his usual gang of people, swooning after him and making him feel like ten men when really in my mind he was no man at all. I soon learned that this man – who I once thought was my friend – did not in fact care if I lived or died. All he cared about was making his money and retaining his popularity. I wished I had never have met him and more than that I wished I had the inner strength to say 'No' all those months ago at the initial party I had gone to.

For now though, here I was.

There was no way out and so in a secluded part of the bar I passed him over the drugs that he'd asked me to bring inside. As soon as he had it I scurried off. I was not interested in hanging around with these people anymore. I didn't like them and I knew if I stayed near them then I would only be convinced to do some more work that I did not want to do.

Now on weekends I started going home on a night time as opposed to staying out all night. I guess being a drug mule helped me see a little bit of sense. What was the point on staying out where I would end up taking more drugs myself and getting in more debt? Then the whole point of doing these drops to the drug dealer was pointless as I was not repaying my debts if I stayed out.

I continued this charade for a few months and during this time I also started working in a factory part-time. I had a little more energy now that I wasn't out the entire weekend and this meant I could start paying bills again. But more importantly, working meant I could not take drugs every single day.

The trouble was that I knew I had more confidence on drugs and I also found that I worked a lot quicker on the factory line if I had got high the night before. My body the next day was still buzzing and so I found I did more work if I was still high.

So getting this job did not solve the problem entirely, but I had definitely cut my addiction right down. By now I had paid quite a big chunk of my drug debt off just by doing some shifts in a factory, but also by carrying drugs on nights out and also by only staying out until midnight or one o'clock, as opposed to through until the next day.

I had started to sort my household bills too and had re-set up my direct debits. My main priority though was getting this drug debt paid, as I just wanted to re build a normal, better life for me and my girl.

I tried to maintain fun time in the house with Abi, despite having next to nothing. It was important there was happy memories for her. We improvised on things we did not have; for example, one when it snowed, we went out sledging on a hoover! I could not afford a sledge, so we made do with what we had. My friend Clare would come around and we would have a laugh sledging on this bloody hoover.

In summer we went to the park and had little picnics, with things that did not cost the earth. Clare would visit me often and if she got money she always tried to help me, and if I got money I would always try and help her. She had her own struggles but she was always there for me.

She knew I took drugs, but she didn't know to what extent; I hid that from her, I hid that from everyone.

I would to this day be lost without Clare. She really was and still is a great friend to me.

By Summer 2008 I was now in my flow.

I had cracked the school runs a lot better purely because I was going out less and I had also mastered paying my debts. I found a way of clearing some of my drug debts and I was, for now at least, surviving.

I was still taking drugs on a weekend but I was not half as bad as I used to be in the previous months. I had more or less cut it out during the week altogether.

I thought I was doing really well until I was asked to carry drugs into a specific new bar. The bar had just opened and it was heaving, it was a squash once inside and you just couldn't move for people. I knew the door staff were new and that security would be extra tight on actually getting into this venue and so I was nervous. My drug dealer – who I still owed a few thousand pounds to – had agreed to wipe off £500 for this drop and I thought, *right Vikki, that's a good chunk off your bill, you can do this.*

I agreed to be there and I agreed to his rules once again, but I knew this was really risky, even more so than before.

Nevertheless, I made it in; luckily for me, a bouncer who knew me had been drafted in to work on this door on this one night and so when I arrived he let me straight in.

I thanked my lucky stars and knew in ten minutes or so I would not be carrying this loot and I would be free to walk back out the door and go home.

But it was easier said than done. In my head all I had to do was retrieve the drugs and pass back to the dealer. The trouble was, amongst all the pushing and shoving to get to the bar area, I somehow managed to lose the entire lot.

Now I had no drugs on me at all.

I'd had 25 bags of pure cocaine on me, with a street value of £700 to £800.

It was now lost, and I panicked.

What the hell was I going to do? I was terrified. I might get *killed* for this.

But I bit the bullet and – in the busiest bit of the bar – I told the dealer what had happened.

Surprisingly it went better than I thought; I wasn't killed, or even beaten up, but I *was* told I now had eight hundred quid added onto my bill, plus interest.

I was now scared and really disappointed with myself. I had only agreed to this stupid drop in order to lose £500 of my own debt, and now I still had it along with an extra eight hundred on top of it.

I walked out of the club and burst into tears.

Was there no end to this bloody madness?

CHAPTER 14: IN A RIGHT MESS

So knowing full well I was in trouble and by now in a really low mood I decided to go to a house party.

Once there and with the happy atmosphere I once again fell back into my ways I was trying to rid myself of and so I figured if you can't beat them then join them and so I got high with everyone else and tried not to think about what had just happened.

My earlier night's mistake was now firmly at the back of my mind. I got engrossed with the new atmosphere and started laughing and joking with the two girls I did know who were there. Everyone else in the room were strangers but strangers with a smile – so for now, that would do for me, I thought.

It was here I first tried Speed and Ketamine (purely because they were offered to me for free and I figured it saved me getting into more debt adding cocaine onto my bill). Both dangerous drugs but put them together and it's complete chaos. Ketamine is a horse tranquilliser used to sedate horses during operations and speed does the exact opposite, it makes your energy levels speed up and your heart go so fast that you can feel it beating through your skin.

I took them both at the same time. Four lines of Ketamine and two tablets of speed.

I was OK for the first twenty minutes but after that everything seemed to stop working. I remember people downing drinks and shouting that the taxis for town were here. I cannot even remember getting into the taxi. I was dragged somehow back to town.

I had no idea who I was with; I just seemed to be following a group I hardly knew. My surroundings were hazy and I felt really sick. I was shivery. It was a bit like flu-like symptoms where you feel really cold but to touch you are really hot and clammy. I also felt like my legs were not even attached to my body. They felt like dead weights that I was just inconveniently dragging along.

Everyone piled into this pub and much to my annoyance they all headed straight to the top floor of the pub. I could hardly get one foot to go in front of the other, let alone climb stairs. I could hear the music and I could hear the tones of voices but I had no idea what anyone was saying or what they were in fact talking about.

I remember two lads either side of me helping me get up the stairs but once there they scuttled off to join the others in the group. I found myself a little space at the top of the balcony overlooking the downstairs bar.

By now I was absolutely freezing but I weirdly had sweat droplets running down my face. My heart was racing, it was going so fast I was actually holding my chest and I knew people were looking at me and I could see their mouths moving and people pointing at me but I didn't care.

I must have looked really odd with one hand half holding me up over a balcony and the other hand clutching my chest. Let them stare, I told myself, because right now there is nothing but nothing I can do about this dire straits situation. I desperately just wanted out of there and to feel better but I could not move to do anything about it.

I just remember clinging to the balcony on the top floor of the night club. I was looking over at the floor beneath me wondering how the hell I was going to get down the stairs because my legs weren't working, when –

BOOM, I hit the floor.

My whole body went from the top floor of the club to the bottom floor.

This was it, I surely had to be dead by now.

I had gone arse over tit over the balcony banister.

I was rushed to hospital. I woke up two days later and I was informed how lucky I was to still be alive.

I was severely dehydrated and I had to have a tooth removed because it was so infected. This was from chewing cocaine. When my nose didn't work I would chew the coke and this made me horrendously grind my teeth. I knew my tooth was rotten but I was too embarrassed to see a dentist, I also couldn't afford it.

I was told by a doctor that the drugs in my system had effectively saved me during the fall because my body was that relaxed that I remarkably didn't even have a broken bone.

I couldn't believe how ironic his sentence was, 'the drugs had saved me'; if only he knew. I was interviewed and I told the people that needed to know that I thought I was spiked.

There was no way on God's green Earth I was going to admit to taking all those drugs by choice, Abi would have been taken from me for sure. Abi was safe at her dad's; he had been told I was in hospital as he was still down as my emergency contact.

I sat in that hospital so ashamed once again. I had really done it this time. I was actually gutted that I had woken up. Now I just had to continue living this bloody nightmare that was called 'my life'.

By summer 2008 I had had enough. My body was exhausted. This person I had become was not me. I desperately needed a break and fast. I needed to change this habit that had gripped me for nearly a year. I was going to be dead soon if things didn't change and that's when I started to think about the Army again.

I knew I was by no way fit or healthy enough for the army but I also knew if I could get in, if I could just find a way then I would be under military discipline and therefore could not touch drugs, after all they were always doing random drug tests. I now needed to execute a plan.

On a sober day I made my way to the Army Careers Office. I explained I wanted to join the Territorial Army (part time army) and that I had previous service. I figured that in order to climb a set of stairs you needed to actually take a step, so here I was chancing my luck and looking for an initial stepping stone. I knew with my previous service in my trade that I would find a way to get in.

I was right; it was not long before I found myself at a reserve unit in Wakefield and where I was collecting my uniform. On the day I went in and signed my paperwork (18 August 2008), I got told what day my medical would be on. Great, I thought. I just know not to do drugs the week before my medical tests, this was all too easy.

Up until that point though I could still come in on Tuesday training nights and earn a bit of money. I started to do this and I ensured I took no drugs on a Monday or Tuesday so I could attend the training sessions on a Tuesday evening.

I could not believe how I managed to get back in and how quickly too. My medical was a few weeks after signing my paperwork, and again I made sure I remained drug-free so all was fine. (There is currently no drug testing to get into the Forces. Yes, on Medicals they take a urine sample but they do not test it for illegal substances. This is how I managed to bypass failing a drug test. There is random drug testing in the Forces but this is done once in and is few and far between).

So now came the hard bit. In December 2008 through to January came the compulsory two-week training camp that you need to pass. Two weeks without drugs seemed a scary thought but I knew I had to do it. I knew I had to try and remain clean for the two weeks in order to get some money in but also to prove to John I could stop taking drugs and that I was worthy of keeping Abi full time.

I was not going to let drugs beat me.

I had somehow survived the year but I knew it was just pure chance.

If I carried on the way I was then Abi would be motherless and my gravestone would merely say 'drug addict mother lives here'.

Time to change.

CHAPTER 15: SURVIVING

I have to say throughout the duration of the two-week course I did not think about drugs once. It was out of sight, out of mind. I was actually enjoying doing something I thought was worthwhile.

I by no means found it easy. My body was messed up and I certainly wasn't the fit girl I used to be. However, with the help of other people I met on the course they somehow pushed me over the finish line every time. They did not know the hurdles I was facing at the time and I think most just assumed I was unfit.

I completed the course and by the end I was actually sad to be going home. Not because I didn't want to see Abi but because I so desperately wanted to remain on the straight and narrow but being back in my drug den would make this rather impossible.

I was right; by Easter 2009 I was back to my regular weekend drug binges and now I had even lied to my best friend Kati about it. I promised her that I was not on drugs and that I was clean but that was not true. I think deep down she knew.

I continued to work on Tuesday evenings at the Army unit but again all the time going out on weekends. I just hoped that no random drug tests would occur because I knew this would put me right back to square one, yet I was that stupid I risked it. It was a shallow and desperate move. It was addiction. No matter how much I wanted to stop I just couldn't.

Again I knew something had to change but I did not know what to do. Also, my little house I was living in now had rats. Not because I was dirty, I had always been a clean and tidy person. I hate dirt, there is no excuse for living in a dirty house, even at my worst my house was always spotless. The rats were getting in through the outhouse that led onto Abi's bedroom. The boiler was kept in Abi's bedroom and they were attracted to the heat of it. Well, so I was told anyway.

I absolute hate rodents, they scare me to death so me and Abi went to stay in a hotel for a few days. I just could not sleep in that house; especially on my French bed that was so close to the floor. The rats were the last straw and I knew right there and then that this was it, it was now or never.

I decided to re-join the Regular Army full time.

Just how the hell was I going to do it with no family nearby to support me with the care of Abi was something I needed to figure out.

With that I rang John. I told him my plan and he was all for it. He knew something had to change. He was getting close to arresting me himself in order to get me to stay off drugs.

I rang my reserve unit and told them I wanted to go back into the army full time. I knew it would be easy because I was already in the reserves. I knew I would not need another medical and I knew they would take me. I contacted my Landlord and not only did I tell him he had rats, I also told him that I was giving up the house and that he could have it back.

I gave myself four weeks to get packed and get back into the army. I decided I would put all my belongings into storage. It would cost me eighty pounds a month but I figured this was a small price to pay to get my life back.

I started going out for more runs. I was still doing drugs on a weekend but I was slowly starting to do less, and that in itself was an achievement.

It wasn't long before I received a phone call telling me they had a start date for Phase Two training for me.

Hang on a minute, I thought, Phase Two training? I was not expecting that, I had stupidly thought I would just go straight back into a unit without doing the training again; but I was soon told that because I had been out the Regular Army for eight years that I would need to re-train. That certainly burst my bubble. That meant twelve weeks with hardly seeing Abi, however I accepted the date and just thanked my lucky stars for this opportunity to once again start afresh.

I knew it was going to be extremely hard. I was effectively about to go cold turkey whilst under training. So 31st May 2009 I found myself saying goodbye to Abi and on my way back to Winchester for Phase Two training, the place I started at eight years previously. The whole four-and-a-half-hour car journey, I cried.

This was going to be tough and – I am not going to lie – even *I* didn't think I was going to do it.

But I did.

CHAPTER 16: BACK IN THE ARMY

Monday 1st June 2009 I was back in the Regulars (my second chance), my first day back in training.

It was surreal to me, being back in the place that I spent 3 months at, 8 years earlier, again trying to sort my life out. This time it was going to be even harder because not only was I trying to sort my life out but I was trying to get clean and stay clean.

So Day 1, let the training commence.

The first day involved testing your fitness levels to ensure that you are fit enough to start the course. A mile and half run, press ups and sits ups followed by full medicals.

Wahooooooo, just what I need, I thought.

My teeth were already starting to chatter because of my come-downs and I was feeling like an emotional wreck. I had just given Abi up technically for twelve weeks; this was the longest I would be without her. I also had in the back of my head that if I did not succeed at this and I failed then I would never get Abi back full-time from John and quite rightly so; however, I did know failure was not an option.

I had nothing to go back to, not even my rat-infested home that I had given up.

So here we go then, I am stood at the start line waiting to be tested on my run, to myself I was shitting it but to others I was smiling. I had to try and pretend I was happy to be here. That I was confident I was going to pass and like I wasn't fazed by it.

I could hear the other people on my course discussing how much they had trained and what their rough run times were. It ranged from 8 minutes 30 seconds right up to 12 minutes. I knew I had to do the run in 12 minutes 30 seconds or I would fail and be put on a re-test, fail again and I would be off the course. I also knew my body was weak. I was constantly freezing, I hadn't been eating correctly, I was withdrawn and tired, my teeth were a mess from grinding them and as for training for the army, well, who was I kidding?! The Army was just an idea that popped into my head a few weeks ago whilst I was off my face on drugs, I never expected to really get in nor did I expect to be stood here now, about to be tested on my fitness levels but here I was; and with that, the signal to start was given and I was off.

Right Vikki, it's time to move your arse, it's time to sweat some of this shit out your system, it's time to prove you are going to take every inch of pain in order to get your daughter back.

I talked to myself the whole way round the course, there were people flying past me but I tried not to let it phase me, I just knew I needed to keep going. A mile in though, and I was knackered. My legs were so weak, who was I kidding? I couldn't do this. I was aching all over.

I stopped and started walking.

Then another female who was not far behind me caught up with me and said 'Come on mate, don't walk.'

I thought to myself 'what the fuck', there are people behind me, I can't be doing that bad and then I thought bless her, this girl has known me two minutes and she was trying to give me encouragement. It was really nice.

With that I started running again, I could soon see the finish line and to my amazement when I crossed it, the fitness instructor called out my time. 11 minutes and 16 seconds. Hang on a minute; did I just hear that right? Did I actually just pass and with over a minute to spare? Was he talking to me?

I couldn't believe it, nor could I believe that there were actually quite a few people behind me.

I had passed. I had done it.

Thank fuck for that.

Now I just needed to get through the medical. I was terrified in case there was any traces of cocaine use in my urine. I thought there would be for sure. There was no way I was going to get away with this. I was nervous.

My name was called up and it was my turn to go through and see the nurse. First my height and weight was checked. Then I had a blood pressure check where I was told it was a little high (I just thought yup, no shit Sherlock, if only you knew why) and then I was queried about my previous medical history.

I was then told to wait in the waiting room for the doctor. I thought great this is it, I am doomed. I have to see the doctor, there's no way I am getting out of this building Scott free.

The doctor called my name and as I sat shuffling in my chair expecting them to suddenly know what I had done, I was merely asked if I had been on medication for my blood pressure and if it had always been high. (In my head I thought, nope it's not always been high but I wish I was high right now). I was told I was quite young to have high blood pressure and asked if I had a bad diet.

I explained I had just been stressed with leaving my daughter and that I had to give up everything to be here. With that the doctor said that it was understandable, and that he would review it in two weeks' time.

I left the doctors room expecting to be called in by a nurse for a urine sample but to my amazement there was nothing. I walked out the Medical Centre and back to my room and I silently cried into my pillow with relief.

I had managed to pull the scariest bits off.

I was starting to think I could actually do this.

CHAPTER 17: SETTLING IN

So now a few weeks into my course and I had made some friends. I shared a room with two other girls. This was not like Phase Two training I did previously where I shared a room with twelve other girls, I was now classed as a re-joining soldier and so I got a bit more privacy because I had done training before.

I was put with two other females who also had previous military experience and who were also slightly older than a new recruit fresh out of training. This was good because we had a slight advantage not being in the main block with the other recruits. We did not get room inspections frequently and we did not get woken up at all hours for stupid things.

To me it was a blessing in disguise. I needed a bit more quiet whilst I was getting myself sorted and I honestly think I would have cracked if I had frequent days of being stood by my bed having someone give me and my kit the once-over.

I was treated like an adult, it's just a shame I did not feel like one.

I didn't even feel human half the time but I couldn't grumble, I was still alive. I was now in a job where I was getting paid monthly and I was now able to start somehow clawing my life back together. It was going to be a long twelve weeks but I had made a start.

I found myself really missing Abi, I thought of her every single day. The guilt for leaving was immense but the guilt for being such a shit mum was even worse. I knew I was doing the right thing by staying here and sorting myself out, however hard that may be. I had made my bed and now it was my time to deal with the consequences. It was time to prove to everyone including myself that I was worthy to be a mother. There was no way I was giving up, however hard it was going to be.

The days in camp were fine because we were always so busy running about from one classroom to another. Between lessons in class, to field-craft lessons, to fitness sessions, to weapon training, to more fitness sessions, I just did not even have time to think. This was very much a good thing but then on the evenings in our free time, I would get so low. I had no one to tell how I was feeling. I was ultimately on my own and so it wasn't long before I started spending more and more time in the bar on camp.

Spending my time at the bar on camp soon made me get talking more to the people on the course. I soon made friends. I soon had got in with a nice group who were younger than me and fitter, but they somehow included me. I was starting to feel accepted.

A few weeks of evening sessions at the bar and having a laugh with the other recruits and it wasn't long before I was starting to feel a bit happier. I now knew that when I was low there was always going to be someone to talk too. This was not like being at home and feeling depressed where you could not just sit and talk to someone, this was like living with a family and they were always there to listen.

Of course the alcohol helped and I never once spoke of my struggles with drink, drugs and depression but what I could talk about without judgement was my debt I had got into and the fact I was doing this for a better life for me and Abi.

I made some really good friendships here and to this day I am still friends with a good couple of people I met on this course. They didn't know it but they helped me succeed in staying to the end.

Without them I would have crumbled.

On my second week in training my best friend's wedding was coming up. I had already let her down before, what with lying about my habit and missing a family funeral for previous Army reserve commitments, so I knew there was no way I could let her down again. She would never ever forgive me, I was a bridesmaid and I owed it to her to be there.

But just getting out of work was going to prove rather difficult.

I begged my training Instructor if I could please go home for the weekend (leaving for weekends on the first three to four weekends in training was not allowed). This particular weekend we were working. There was no weekend off. I was powerless and I had no idea what to do. How the hell was I going to tell Kati that I could not attend?

I begged and begged the instructors a little more and to my dismay I was granted the one day off. I was allowed to attend the wedding but I had to drive straight back from Wakefield straight after the ceremony. I was given a curfew of 8pm. Great, no relaxing and chilling time with my best mate then, no getting drunk; in fact, no drinking at all. Just up at the crack of dawn for a long drive there and then I would have to leave around tea time for my long drive back.

I was slightly disheartened but I was glad I didn't have to tell her I that I couldn't go at all.

When I arrived, I had my hair done at her sister's house, my feet were a mess from all the runs, I had blisters and cuts everywhere and so my bridesmaid's shoes looked hideous on my feet with all the plasters. Nevertheless, I was there, and so was Abi.

I was over the moon. My two favourite people. I was getting to spend time with them both but not only that, I was sober. They hadn't seen me sober in a long time. I had a lovely day, Kati looked beautiful and I cried with happiness for her. I was so relieved I got to be part of her special day but I was also so sad I couldn't stay for it all, I was ridden with guilt, I was a shit mate and I knew it. I missed her cutting the cake and her first dance, I missed the night-time fun, I missed us having a dance together and me getting to cuddle her in her beautiful princess dress. Leaving the wedding venue, I knew she was crushed I was leaving but I really couldn't stay. I could see the disappointment in her eyes and I could also see how sad Abi was that I was going.

I got into my car and I sobbed for a good thirty minutes. I felt so guilty, I felt like fucking the army off and not going back at all but I knew if I did that, that in a month's time I would be back to square one; and so with that, and with a heavy heart, I set off back to Winchester.

After a few weeks into training we were allowed our weekends to ourselves. This was great as it meant I could drive back to Wakefield and see Abi. The only downside was it was a near five hour drive each way and I had nowhere to go.

I had no home to go back to and I had no family nearby I could go see or take Abi to. This meant that I could only afford to see her three to four weekends out of the twelve weeks training because each time I had to drive miles for her and then pay for a hotel for the weekend. I already had no money because of my debts. However, seeing Abi was more important.

I did what I could. The weekends I got to see Abi were amazing, I had been off drugs, I was slowly getting fitter and I was actually starting to function again. These weekends were to be the happiest weekends in a long time; weekends where she would actually see me smile and not cry.

We loved chilling in the hotel, snuggling up and watching films and TV. She would tell me how she was doing at school and I would tell her how it wasn't long until we got our new house and mummy was coming home for good.

Trouble was, I had no idea where home was going to be. We did not find out where we were getting posted to until week eleven.

Twelve weeks in training doesn't sound long but when your heart is pining for someone you dearly love and miss and when your body and mind is broken, the twelve weeks felt like twelve years. The drive back to camp on a Sunday was always demure. I hated saying goodbye, not knowing when I could afford another weekend in a hotel. I always cried the whole way back. My whole wage was more or less swallowed up by debts, I had even agreed to pay back my drug dealer monthly because I did not like the idea of doing all this and then always fear that someone was looking for me.

I think during training I was lucky if I was left with thirty pounds a month to myself. However, at least here I was not getting into more debt, I was not taking drugs and my daughter was safe. The girls in my room would always arrive back to our shared room on a Sunday full of lovely things they had bought on their shopping sprees and I couldn't help but feel extremely envious. I knew I did not deserve to be jealous, I had put myself in this mess, so I would just have to wait my turn until I too could buy nice new things.

For now though, I was happy with a roof over my head, air in my lungs and this new chance.

I knew I had to just look at the bigger picture.

CHAPTER 18: <u>MOVING ON</u>

I continued training, I continued keeping up the pretence that everything was ok and I successfully made it to the end.

It was by no means easy. I had my ups and downs, I had irritable mood swings, I had struggled emotionally on a daily basis but I had done it. I passed the course.

I had made such good friends here. They really did help me feel alive again. The weekends when we were allowed out but I couldn't afford to go and see Abi I would stay with some of the other girls on camp and we would go to the cinema and bars and stuff and I really did start to feel like me again. I was a functioning adult enjoying life without drugs again. I was so pleased with myself. I was always giggling these days and always happy. I actually think my peers at some points thought I *was* on drugs because now I was like an overexcited child in a sweet shop. I was so smiley. They had no idea why, but I knew.

I now had everything to live for.

First step, get an address for my new army house and plan for Abi to come home. It was an amazing feeling telling John I had done it. Deep down, I didn't think we would be having this conversation but now we were.

I had been posted to an Artillery unit in Catterick and my start date was 31st August 2009. I was given an army quarter and now I had a home.

On 5th September 2009 I moved into my army house. I will always remember this date because it marked my new start with my seven-year-old.

I arranged for my furniture to be delivered from storage and I made full use of my relocation leave spending time with Abi and making our first house in a long time into a home.

I didn't have a lot of furniture but luckily with the Army you can rent furniture with the house and so I did this. It wasn't long before I had made it nice for us and soon we had settled living back together.

Catterick is an hour's drive to Wakefield so I wasn't close enough to fall back into bad crowds but I was still close enough for Abi's dad to visit or for us to drive and meet half way for shared custody. I was also still close enough to see my real friends.

I started at my new post and again every day I had a smile on my face.

Why wouldn't I? I had succeeded in something huge, I had won my daughter back and I was now in my own little house earning my own money.

Yes, I still had a lot of debt but I could manage it and I could think clearly without being ruled by poison. Again though, my new work mates at this new unit thought I was on drugs. People would question why I was always so happy and bubbly. If I got shouted at or disciplined in my line of work I would be stood smiling.

This got me into a lot of trouble. It used to wind my seniors up but I honestly was so bloody happy. I had no idea what people were getting their fucking knickers in a twist for over things that were very simple to fix. One of my new bosses would go mad if the shredder bin wasn't emptied or if the tea towels in the staff room weren't cleaned and to me I would just think Jesus, in the grand scheme of things is this really worth getting angry about?

I did really struggle with military discipline at first. I just didn't understand why people were so hot headed over simple things. I also didn't get why some people had let their rank get to their head.

It wasn't long before I was in trouble. In fact, I think it took all of two months.

Basically I was made duty clerk. This is where you are on 24 call for any emergencies over the silent hours; if someone needs an emergency train ticket, if welfare needs some emergency contact details, if someone gets injured, etc. So being on duty clerk you also had to stay in RHQ – regimental headquarters – until the last person had left the building. So boring, I hated it.

On one particular duty (I had not done many and was still learning the ropes), I was waiting in the building for an Officer to finish but he was taking ages. He called me to his office to go find a Brent Key. He told me it was in the safe. Right, Ok, I'll go get it then Sir, so off I trot. I got to the safe, I could not see a key anywhere in there. So off I trot back downstairs, tell this to him.

By now he starts to get a little angry and he tells me again that it is in the safe and where to look. Right Sir, I'll go back and look.

So once again off I go, back upstairs and I have another look. But nope, it definitely is not in there. I knew he was going to be angry but hey-ho, let's go tell him, so I go back down the stairs and tell him there is no key in that safe.

So now the Officer gets out of his seat, says to me if he has to come up there and look for the key himself there will be trouble.

Right, okay, 'Fuck this,' I thought.

I went back upstairs and sat at my desk for ten minutes. Then my office phone went. It was him. He tells me he is coming up to look in the safe and that I'm to stand by if the key is in there. I replied that's fine Sir, come and look. I was confident there was no bloody key in the safe. So in he walks, opens the safe and the first thing he pulls out is a little black stick. He starts ranting and raving and telling me I'll be on duty from now until Christmas for this. In my head I was thinking 'Fuck you', why didn't you just tell me you wanted a little black stick? I guess he didn't realise this was my first Army unit since basic training and he just presumed I knew what a Brent key was. I honestly though had no idea that a Brent Key was a little plastic stick that you insert into the side of a phone. I had just spent ages looking for a key, something that to me is metal and not stick-like at all.

He had made me fuming. He had wasted my time by going up and down the stairs, he clearly knew I had no idea what I was looking for and could have easily described it better, more still he could have got it himself knowing full well I was struggling with what it actually was.

Now I was getting a bollocking for something that was not even my fault. My temper flared up like a red rag to a bull and so I thought that's it, the first opportunity I get, I'm off. It wasn't long before he went to the toilet and the minute he did I stuck a note on his desk along with the duty clerk keys so he could lock up himself.

I simply wrote, if I am not good enough for your duty then do your own bloody duty clerk. Here's the keys, I'm off on the piss.

Then with that I proceeded down to the block and cracked open a bottle of wine. He rang me a few times on the duty clerk phone but I told him I was not coming back to be spoken to like that, he made me nervous and I was now so angry. In my head I thought I was worth more than this. What right did he have to make me feel that bloody nervous and to make me feel that silly? There was no way I was going back there and being his lap dog for the rest of the evening and so I carried on drinking in the block with a couple of people I am still friends with now.

I knew it was the wrong thing to do but on this occasion I did not do the right thing. To know whether you are doing the right thing, the army has what is known as the Service Test –

Have the actions or behaviour of an individual adversely impacted or are they likely to impact on the efficiency or operational effectiveness of the Army (unit)?

In this case, I knew I would have failed.

CHAPTER 19: <u>REPERCUSSIONS</u>

As suspected, the Officer could not wait to grass me up to my boss for my failure to complete my duty. I knew he was morally obliged to report my behaviour but still I was annoyed and sulking. I knew I was wrong for not returning and I knew it was a serious offence and that I deserved what was coming but in my own defence it was something that I would not have done if he hadn't been an arse in the first place.

Still, here I was stood in front of my boss getting a bollocking. I wasn't really given a chance to explain and being in this tiny office getting shouted at whilst hung over meant I wasn't sure if I wanted a chance. I just needed to get out of there. I was put on a three-month warning order. This is where for three months if I stepped out of line I could be charged or, worse still, posted out of the unit and I knew that would mean moving Abi again, something I did not want to do.

I took my three-month warning order letter and stuck it in the shredder.

There was no way I was sitting and looking at the thing for the next three months, it would only bring me down. I knew it could have been a lot worse and I could have been charged for insubordination so I guess I just had to get on with it now. I honestly felt these people had no idea about real-life problems in the real world; I could not hold a grudge over their sheer ignorance. Karma will get them I thought. So I continued to try and settle into the Regiment.

Daily office life though was good, I had a great working partner, she taught me loads. If I was stuck she would help, if I was getting too lairy she would give me press-ups in the office and tell me it was for my own good. If I was getting grief off the lads that came into the office she would tell them to wind their necks in. She was a great mentor.

I, however, sometimes could be rude to her. I was very up and down with my moods. Sometimes I would be over-the-top happy and then other times I would be so angry and moody that you could cut the atmosphere with a knife. How she didn't kill me I will never know.

We had one massive fallout and when my bosses got wind of it I felt like she had massively betrayed me. I couldn't understand why she had told them. Little did I know, that is was for my own good. My bosses spoke to me this time trying to understand what the hell was going on between me and my mentor. It was not long before we soon made friends again and everything was sorted.

It was from here it was agreed I would join the Cross Country Team. They told me more fitness meant a better working environment and that I could run off my high energy levels doing this and that also when I was low or moody it would release happy endorphins. I accepted it and with that I started training with the Cross Country Team.

No idea why they thought I was a good runner. Yes, I was tall and trim, with long skinny legs but I was by no way fit. I had only been drug-free since May 2009. It hadn't even been six months but I thought fuck it, I'll do their stupid, poxy Cross Country, I'll show them.

Now training was hard. With every ounce of my heart I hated it. It was so hard at first and I always seemed to hold up the team. I was always dragging at the back. I would like to say it got easier but I can safely say it never did. Even when my fitness did improve I still struggled. Still, it gave me a focus but more importantly it gave me time out the office. I was getting paid to run. That was a perk in itself.

So by January 2011 I was now taking part in Cross Country races around the UK with the Regimental running team. I had also paid £4,000 of debt off. I still had a huge £22,000 to go but I had made a good star; well, I thought so, anyway.

I think after my rent had been taken out of my wages along with my council tax, I was earning then around £1,100. Out of that money I was paying £950 a month on debts. Then £50 each on my current gas and electric. That was a total cost of £1,150, this meant I had £50 a month left to live on. All my child benefit and working tax credits went on paying childcare for Abi.

I actually now have no idea how I managed. My car was always running on vapour and I was forever living on market value beans and toast.

I could have taken the easy option and gone to Army Welfare and declared myself bankrupt but I knew that had implications of being a Clerk in the Forces and I was scared about losing my job that I had worked so hard for.

I also knew I still carried my ex-husband's surname and we still had a few financial ties, I did not want to drag his name through it all and risk him losing his credibility for something I had done. This was my debt and there was no way I was going to take the easy option. For now, going without would be my life long lesson about debt and the stark realities of the doom and gloom it brings.

CHAPTER 20:

NEW YEAR – THE START OF 2010

I was now starting to get fitter, I was now starting to get my life on track and I was now starting to settle into the Army way of life. I had a purpose to get up in the morning again and things to do that fulfilled my days.

The fitness was working quite well with my up and down moods and I had got a good home life routine with Abi.

The thing was, I was still really struggling with money.

I would see all my work colleagues out drinking and buying new cars, new clothes, new kit and so on, and I couldn't even afford branded labels in the supermarket. Nevertheless, I was a damn sight better off now than I was a year ago. I had come a long way. I got stuck into the army way of life and kept my head down and then, out of nowhere, came a man.

He was more senior than me but I knew he liked me. We were in the same working Company in the Army and so we definitely could not be seen to like each other, mixing with higher ranks was not the done thing.

Regardless though, before we knew it we were messaging back and forth and it wasn't long after that, that he started coming round to my house with bottles of wine.

We would talk until all hours and then go to work the next day like we hardly knew each other, careful not to give other people the knowledge of what was really going on. I knew this man was married with two children; however, he told me the marriage was over. I believed him because he never wore a wedding ring.

I now loved going to work, I loved seeing him and I loved the thrill of the chase.

He made going to work a little more worthwhile and made me happy. Valentine's Day 2010, he left an engagement ring box in my car with one Rolo in it. It made me smile. I had forgotten what it was like to feel like this. I had been separated from John for over five years now and yes, I had the odd date here and there or very short relationships, but this felt different.

By spring we were dating and by summer I was very much in love.

He played Regimental Rugby and had previously been a boxer, he was well respected at the unit and in a weird way I felt protected. For the first time I felt like someone was going to look after me and I had nothing more to fear.

With a romance now on the cards it was not long before our superiors got wind of the fact we were a couple and due to the fact I was the last one into the Company that we worked in, I was now the first one out. I was moved to another office on camp. This was fine I thought, there was no way we should be working together all day and going home together, to me that was not healthy. I was just happy I didn't get posted out of the Regiment altogether. We booked a late summer getaway to Benidorm on our own and for the first time in years I was settled.

It was not long though until the cracks started to form; he drank a lot and I was now drinking a lot too. Now he was disappearing on weekends but I was told he was going to see his children. I always felt like there was something missing but I was so in awe of him that I didn't dare push my boundaries. He seemed good with my daughter and he kept me from feeling lonely, he was someone to talk too on a night time, there was no way I could risk losing him.

We were allowed to go to Germany together on adventure training and I loved it. Our secret was out and we could sit and have a laugh with our other work colleagues on the journey over. As much as I loved the Germany trip it was here we had our first major fall-out. We were drunk and I got so mad with him I poured a drink over his head; something I would later regret as we argued for the rest of the trip.

I still cannot to this day recall why I did that or what the argument was about. By Christmas 2010 we were getting ready for all the Christmas parties they have on Army camps during this season and I remember this time as a happy one. I was still struggling with money but now I had a little bit of help financially when I needed it, someone to do a food shop or put petrol in my car. I felt like a real couple who was sharing the grown up bills.

I was no longer battling everything alone.

By 2011 Abi was not enjoying her school. In fact, she hated it. She didn't have that many friends and we were starting to clash. She was now eight and would by nine in October.

I was also starting to resent the fact my partner could always go to the pub after work and go on out on weekends without me and I worried so much that he wouldn't come home and I would be back to being on my own with all my struggles. So with this in mind I mentioned to Abi about joining boarding school.

I by no means wanted rid of her but I figured she might like it, she would get a better education and I would still see her on the odd mid-week evenings and also weekends. She agreed to take a look around and go for a trial and to my dismay she loved it. I applied for her funding through the Army (this is called the Continuity of Education Allowance where soldiers who do not stay in one location for their whole military career are allowed to apply for funding in order to keep the child in one place and settled throughout their schooling period) and by September 2011 my daughter was moving out and starting boarding school.

When the day came for her to leave I was crushed. Completely heartbroken. I couldn't believe I was willingly doing this and I couldn't believe one of my reasons was a completely selfish one. I wanted to concentrate on my relationship because I was scared of rejection. Abi was brilliant though, her first few weeks she always sounded happy on the phone and I had no worries whatsoever that I had done the wrong thing by her.

She loved sharing a room with other girls and she loved the fact the classrooms were smaller and she got more time with the teachers. She loved her boarding parents and she loved all the fun activities they did on an evening on a weekend.

I, on the other hand, was lost. I started to crumble. I was angry all the time. I was angry at myself for sending her there, I was angry that now I had sent her there to spend more time with my partner yet he did not really seem focused on us, it was still the Army, rugby and drinking with his mates that was his main priority. This angered me a lot. We rowed constantly.

Christmas 2011 and Abi was coming home. I was so excited I booked the three of us a holiday to Lanzarote. Little did I know that this would be the last really happy memory of the three of us together.

I couldn't afford the holiday by any means but I was desperate to spend time as a family and make a real fuss of Abi. I had missed her. We had a lovely family holiday. I stood at the edge of the clifftop overlooking the sea and at that moment I felt completely in love and I wished with all my heart I was about to get engaged.

A girl can dream.

It never happened though and we all eloped back to the hotel.

CHAPTER 21: MENTALLY ILL

By summer 2011 I was exhausted. I was by now sure my partner was seeing someone else although I had no proof and I was racked with guilt over putting Abi into boarding school, despite her loving it. I felt like I failed as a mother yet again. I was running about like mad in the army and had really pulled my socks up so much so I had been selected for promotion.

On 29 Jul 2011 I passed my promotion course and I was happy about this but at the same time I mentally felt lost. I was struggling. By Christmas this year I had a full mental breakdown which resulted me in taking some time off work. I was referred to the mental health team for soldiers and I soon had a Councillor. However, no matter what he said just did not help. It was like he was speaking to me trying to help but nothing he was saying was sinking in. I would describe it like living as a bat. I could hear what he was saying but all I could see was darkness. There was sound but I had no vision. The thought of going back to work made me panic. I felt like everyone was laughing at me, I felt like everyone knew there was something wrong and more importantly I felt like everyone knew what my partner was up to but me.

I was lost, paranoid and back on a road of self-destruction through drink. My mood swings were now a nightmare to manage and I hated what I was doing to myself. I hated feeling like this. Regardless of me being sick he had put his name down for winter skiing and off he went for near a month pursuing his leisure interests. I felt alone. I had no support and I didn't like to discuss with my Wakefield friends what I was going through because I was sure they would think oh God, Vikki is going back downhill again. I didn't want to worry them.

January 2012 I went back to work. I was starting to feel a little better and I knew my partner would be back soon and things would be okay. I figured New Year, New Start. Once he was back he spoke about marriage. This certainly perked me up. He had missed me, well so I thought anyway. He had pushed for a divorce with his ex-wife and I was happy we were making plans.

I started preparing and we went to see wedding venues. We found a gorgeous little venue in Scarborough and despite having very little money I paid £500 deposit to secure the wedding date of 5 August 2012. I now had a new focus. I was driven again.

I went about my ways trying on dresses and it was not long until I found my dream dress. Again I paid a deposit. By March I had made a wedding plan and list, I had secured a venue, bought a dress, found rings, prepared my hen do plans for a summer trip to Magaluf and was slowly getting excited.

Due to all the excitement, I hadn't noticed my period was late. Was I pregnant?

No I couldn't be, I was always careful with my pill.

To my amazement though, on Sunday 4th March I did a test and it was positive.

I sat in the bathroom staring at the test. I was happy. I couldn't believe it, not only was I getting married but we were now expecting our first baby together. I ran through to the bedroom to tell my partner hoping he would be as happy as me but the reality was, he never said a word. For the rest of the evening he remained quiet.

I told myself he was just shocked with the news and by the morning everything would be okay. I was wrong.

Monday 5th March 2012 – the day my world crumbled.

We went to work as normal. The eight-mile car journey to camp was spent sitting in silence. When we arrived I said, 'See you at tea time,' trying to act as normal as possible.

Little did I know that this morning was the last morning ever we would travel to work together.

In fact, this morning would be that last time ever we would be a couple.

CHAPTER 22: ON MY OWN AGAIN

I arrived home that evening to find all my partners stuff had gone.

He had been back to the house through the working day and had taken not only his things but some of my things. I frantically starting calling him, but nothing. I was at my wits end with worry. I told myself to just go to bed and that tomorrow I could see him at work and we would sort everything.

Only the next day at work, he didn't want to talk to me.

He told me he was leaving and he didn't want to be with me anymore. He told me it was over and we just weren't working and more than that he did not want a baby.

I felt like I had just been kicked in the stomach.

Then I started receiving messages from what I thought was his ex-wife. How wrong was I? It turned out he had been going home to her most weekends and they were still a couple. I had no idea. By now I looked like I had ruined another family's life through no fault of my own. I could not understand it because I had met his children, surely that meant his wife already knew about me. How could they still be a couple?

My head was in a right mess. I had no idea how after over two years I had not realised all this before. I told myself he would just need to calm down over the shock of having a child together; I convinced myself he would come back. I tried my best to get to work and raise a smile but it was hard.

By now everyone on camp knew I was expecting but worse than that, he had gone round the whole Regiment and told everyone I had cheated. I could not believe it. The whole time he had been going back to his wife and had been stringing me along but yet somehow it was me that was meant to have cheated? He convinced nearly everyone that the baby was not his. I was broken. My head was a complete mess. I didn't know who I could trust. His birthday came and went in April but he still would not take my calls. I was that much in love with him that despite him walking out on me and despite him spreading rumours and despite him still going back to his wife on weekends that I still sent him a birthday card. I never got a reply back. No acknowledgement. Nothing.

He had left me with payday loan debt and would not even discuss re-payments of this. Again, I could have asked to get them written off but I was scared of the impact this would have on my job being a Clerk.

I was starting to realise it really was over and that I was on my own with this pregnancy. The heartache was unbearable. I had my hen do booked for May 2012 and with the love of my good friends they convinced me still to go, that the break might do me good. I agreed to go. Instead of a hen do party it was to be a celebration of getting rid of a man that emotionally hurt me.

The whole holiday I had loads of things whizzing through my head, could I afford another baby on my own, could I do this all on my own, would he come back when the baby was born if I kept it, would he financially support me if I kept it, would he come to my antenatal appointments, did he ever love me at all, what about Abi how was I going to tell her my partner who she had grown close to was not coming back, would he help me buy the baby things?

The list of thoughts was endless, so along with the fact I could not drink on holiday with my friends and that I dreadfully missed him, I found it hard to even raise a smile. My friends were getting annoyed with me feeling blue but I was heartbroken, there was no two ways about it. How would I get past this?

The holiday was not an enjoyable one; although I was grateful to be with my friends I just felt lost.

On my return home and out of sheer desperation I contacted him and asked him to come with me for a termination. This time, he replied. He agreed to take me.

In my heart of hearts, I did not want a termination but I was that desperate to talk to him I would have done or said anything. The morning came to go to the hospital and as discussed by text message he turned up to pick me up. The atmosphere in the car was horrendous, neither one of us spoke and I so desperately wanted him to see me. I so desperately wanted him to tell me he loved me and he was sorry, but it never came.

We spent the whole car journey in silence; he did not even ask if I was okay. I was about to go through a termination for his sake and he couldn't even find it in his heart to ask how I was.

It was here I started to realise he was heartless. In the hospital waiting room I was trying so hard to get him to look at me. I needed him to see the sorrow in my eyes. I needed him to see the pain and heartache I was going through. He never looked at me once.

My name was called; it was time.

The doctor closed the curtain and asked me to undress from the waist down. I did this and propped myself up on the hospital bed. I was told I would be awake for the procedure but sedated and that I would be given pain relief. He put an air mask over my face. I lay back and with tears running down my face, I thought I was ready.

The doctor stopped and asked if I needed more time.

It was then at this very point that I realised this was not what I wanted. I was doing this to please a monster I thought I loved. He was no man if he could sit there in the waiting room without a care in the world as to what emotional upset he was putting me through after ever everything.

I got dressed and walked out to the waiting room where he was waiting. This was the first time he smiled. He thought I had done it. He thought I had got rid of our baby.

Once in the car I burst into tears and told him I couldn't do it. I was expecting him to tell me it would be okay. He said nothing. Instead he looked at me with disgust.

At that moment then I knew there was no going back and in seven months' time I would greet my new baby and prove this man was the dad and that I never once cheated.

It would be the longest wait of my life.

CHAPTER 23: MENTAL BATTLE

Once again I had a breakdown; it was so severe I stopped eating, I was having panic attacks and I just wanted to die. I was alone again and I was panicking. I was scared.

Normally when I felt uneasy I could turn to drink but this time I couldn't, I was pregnant. It wasn't just my life at risk but I had a gift of an unborn baby to protect.

I was lost and at rock bottom, I did not turn up for work and when a work colleague saw the state of me I was taken to hospital.

I was now in a mental health unit in Darlington. I would spend the next two to three weeks here. I felt so ashamed to be here.

Although there is no real shame in it, I was very mindful of the fact that now all my army peers would really think I was mental. Despite on my good days being a fully functioning adult and if I do say so myself a good clerk, I knew my fellow workers would not remember that, they would only see me as the way I am now, broken.

I was always willing to help others and go that extra mile to ensure they left my office as if I have done everything I possibly could to help them. Being in hospital meant I had ruined it all. Well in my mind anyway.

I feared I would never be able to claw back my career after this and without the army, where did that leave me? Jobless, homeless and probably children-less. Without the army I wouldn't be able to pay the rest of my debt off and at this point I had just under £10,000 to go.

I had worked so hard paying as much as I could back. My previous drug dealers were repaid and I now only had three more debts to repay. A stark contrast to 2009 when I had over seventeen creditors and near £27,000 to repay.

The more I thought about the mess I now found myself in, the more I panicked. More than anything though, all I could think about was Abi being taken off me for good. Although she did not know what was happening and was perfectly fine in boarding school I just couldn't help but think she would never be allowed to mine again unsupervised. I had ruined all my hard work. I had managed to survive a drink and drug battle and get through basic training without alarming the authorities but now all because of one man's actions I could face losing my daughter and my unborn baby.

This for me was the pits. I had had enough. I spent endless days laid in the hospital bed praying he would text and apologise and that all this would stop. He, on the other hand, was in Germany on adventure training, loving life, still denying the fact he had a baby on the way, still insisting to everyone I was a cheat.

It was a complete and utter nightmare. I cried for hours and hours on end and the nurses had no idea how to console me. They eventually took my phone off me because staring at it and waiting for him to text was not doing me any good. To them I must have really looked 'mental' but nobody knew how I felt. Nobody understood the pain I was going through.

A few days in and a couple of my army bosses came to visit me. They knew me well as we were all on the Cross Country Team together. They knew my whole sordid story about my so-called partner and although I don't think they believed I hadn't cheated I was just so glad to see a face I recognised but more than that they assured me I was not in trouble. I knew through my time at this Regiment that I had been a pain in the arse to them with my constant highs and lows but I genuinely think they cared. They were actually lovely to me on the visits and despite their harsh exterior at work I started to think if they hadn't have visited me and assured me I was not in trouble then I don't think I would have gone back at all.

In fact, I think I would have pushed for a medical discharge. I am so glad I did not.

In hospital I would see Councillors on a daily basis and they assured me I was not mad. I told them my whole sordid story and they said I was by no means 'mad'. They said most people would have a breakdown going through all that. I was assured I would get better but more importantly they did not fear for my children's safety.

I could still be a mum. That's all I needed to hear. I lived merely to provide for Abi and to make sure I was there so she did not have half the battles I had. I was going to be allowed to keep my unborn baby too, I just needed time to get better first. Hearing that really did perk me up and soon I started eating again.

I was glad I didn't have my phone and I was glad he never came to visit me in the hospital. It would have probably given him great satisfaction to see me in a mess like that. I was too proud to let this break me. I was determined to get mentally fit and get better again. I had to; I had a baby on the way. It would need me because it was going to be me and me alone that would look after it.

I knew I could do it; I just needed to come up with a plan.

Now, making plans when you are mentally struggling is not the easiest of tasks. This would normally take a mentally strongminded person an hour maybe two; for me though, this plan was to take me over two weeks. Still, I got there in the end.

I continued making daily progress and I continued seeing the Councillors. They really did help.

Soon I was allowed to walk to the shops on my own and was trusted enough to come back. Sounds so daft but they need to access risks and that I was not contemplating suicide.

I made friends with another patient in there and although I really did think she was past help some days, on her good days she was so nice and you would never have known there was anything wrong with her. If it wasn't for our surroundings I would have forgotten we were both in a mental health unit.

I spent my time in there talking to her and listening to her troubles and I guess knowing I was not the only one that had had a lifelong battle, I somewhat felt comforted. Very sad fact that someone else's upset gave me some comfort. I wished she had not been hurt but then on the other hand I was realising I was not the only one with problems.

I spent a lot of time in hospital alone. It took me ages to actually get my head around where I was. I would sit doing jigsaws for hours on end just as I did as a child at my granddad's house. I wished with all my heart he was sat with me now helping me not only put my jigsaw together but helping *me* be put back together.

My dad came to visit me. Although it was very strained purely because I am not quite sure he knew what to say but also because of the fact I was embarrassed he was seeing me in here.

My mum had offered to come but I asked her not to. I didn't want her seeing me in here and I didn't want to cause her any undue stress. I knew it would upset her.

I was grateful for my dad's visit but when he left I cried again for hours. I was ashamed.

Although I couldn't help the fact that I needed help, I also felt such a failure. All I ever wanted to do was make both my parents proud and I seemed to fall at every hurdle. I hated myself. I hated looking in the mirror and seeing a weak woman looking back at me. I needed to find a way to get my strength back.

I told myself to give it time.

On my last week in hospital, I felt my baby kick for the first time. I was overwhelmed with emotion.

Despite all my emotional turmoil, my baby was still alive and kicking.

That in itself was a gift. I knew what I needed to do. I needed to get out of hospital and prepare for my new baby. This baby was brought to me for a reason and there was no way I was going to fail it. Not a chance.

It was time to go home.

I was ready.

CHAPTER 24:

PREGNANCY AND THE ARMY

I found the first few nights back at home so strange. It was so quiet. There was no one shouting or screaming in the middle of the night. There was no one singing Christmas songs in the height of summer, there was no one shouting at the chefs because they didn't like the food, there was no one in my living room telling stories, there were no doctors or nurses asking if I was okay, in fact there was no one at all. It was just me and my unborn baby.

I spent the next few months alone. Yes, I went back to work and yes, I tried to act as normal as possible around my work colleagues, but I did not trust a soul. Most people knew where I had been and I was paranoid of what camp thought about me so I hardly spoke of my feelings to anyone and only when I got home on an evening and closed the door behind me would I talk to my unborn baby and explain that if I wasn't pregnant, I don't think I would be here, my unborn baby was going to keep me alive until I got over this blip fully.

I found out I was having another girl and I was over the moon. Me and my girls against the world, I thought. I would sing to her on a night time and promise that by the time she arrived I would be in a lot better position and that I would be a better mummy.

I spent most of my evenings in silence or playing music quietly. I wanted the house calm, I did not want to scare my unborn baby and I also wanted to find me again, only quiet time could do this.

My ex remained on the camp I worked in and if he saw me he would walk in another direction. I asked welfare to arrange a meeting because I wanted my stuff back that he had taken and although he was ordered to give it back, I still to this day never got it. 'Stuff it', I thought, he can have it. It's only stuff.

I continued to try hold my head high despite everyone thinking this baby was someone else's. The only way to get through it was knowing that the truth would come out in the end. I had no idea how he had the audacity to call me a cheat after what he had done but also if he had really known me at all he would know I was extremely shy about my body. I mean, my boobs were literally hitting the floor, why on earth would I want to get naked with someone else? Yes, on my good days I was fun-loving and outgoing but Christ, that didn't make me a cheat. I was so happy I had found someone in the first place, why would I jeopardise this?

Still, only I knew this. It was me against a Regiment who had been brainwashed by him. June to December was the longest six months of my life. I had now been at this Army unit over three years. I had arrived September 2009 and it was now September 2012. Most clerks only do three years at a unit and then they are re-posted, so I knew after the birth of my baby and after maternity leave I would be getting posted to another unit. This was a good thing, it meant yet again another new start. It would be exactly what I needed.

The only thing was, I needed to make sure the army thought I was mentally fit enough to stay in the forces and after my stint in hospital I knew this was going to be a hard task. Every day I went to work trying to hide the pain I was going through. We had an inspection coming up and all my seniors were stressing. I was trying my best not to stress because I knew they were looking for signs of me crumbling. It was hard. My baby was due in December but it was agreed that I would go on maternity leave after the inspection. I think they were scared in case I went off the rails again.

In October 2012 I was released to go on leave and I served my last day at this Regiment. I felt relieved but also a little bit sad. I had started at this unit only three years previously with high hopes. I aimed to pay off my debt and get settled and now I felt more unsettled than ever. I was so nervous for my future. I had no idea where I would be getting posted to after my maternity leave and I had no idea how I would cope being a single parent of two.

Only time would tell.

December 7th, and I had really bad pains. I knew it was the start of labour.

My birthing partner Michelle was spending her last two days with her husband before he returned to his work in Iraq and I really didn't want to take her away from him for longer than I should. This was their time together, it was precious. All my other friends from camp would surely help but when it came to it I couldn't get hold of anyone. I drove myself to hospital. I was extremely uncomfortable but someone had to do it.

I arrived and the midwife confirmed I was in the start of early labour, she explained I could either stay in or go home. I thought that after that drive alone, there was no way I was chancing going home. What if I couldn't drive myself back? There was no one at my house to help me and I would just be stuck panicking by myself. So I decided to stay.

Other ladies in the ward came and went but yet my labour seemed to be taking ages to actually progress. At around eleven that night finally my mucus plug came away and at that point I knew it wouldn't be long until I met my baby. Yes, I was in a little bit of pain but I was too excited to care, I was in the right place and had people caring for me, all I had to do now was prepare to push. I opted not to call my birthing partner until I really needed to.

By the time I needed to it was four in the morning. Michelle was on her way and so was my baby. This labour was not like my first one. With Abi it all happened in a matter of minutes, this one I was just pushing and pushing but the little bugger was stuck.

However, five hours later and she was here. On 8th December at 9.11am, I gave birth to Amelia Hope. She was a whopping 10lbs and the midwife said it was no wonder she got stuck, she had broad shoulders. When she came out she looked like a scrunched up little munchkin. She was so beautiful and I couldn't believe she was mine.

I was still a little bit out of it with gas and air but my birthing partner did a fab job of getting her dressed and sorting her out whilst I came round a bit.

Abi arrived to meet her baby sister and it was the moment I had dreamed of for months.

Me and my girls together forever. I was so proud. I cried with happiness. Amelia's sperm donor – as I now though of my ex – was informed I was in labour, but he wasn't bothered. In fact, on checking afterwards by joint friends I can confirm the pub was more important than the birth of his daughter. His loss. She was amazing. She was beautiful. She was perfect and there was nowhere else I would rather be.

Due to her being such a big baby I had to stay in hospital overnight. I didn't mind. I was only going to sit and stare at her anyway so it would make no difference where I was. I don't think I slept at all that day. I spent all day looking at her and taking pictures. It was an amazing feeling. I was happy.

The next day she had her hospital checks and we were free to go home. I was so excited, but so nervous in case I did anything wrong. I didn't want people judging my solo parenting skills and I felt like everything I did was under scrutiny. I wrapped her up nice and warm and placed her in her car seat. We headed off to collect Abi and together the three of us went home.

There are no words to describe how content I felt. This was it; I was a mum who had been given a second chance not to mess up this little life but to continue righting any wrongdoings from my time with Abi. I was not going to fail.

From now on, my children were my world and nothing would stop me or get in my way. We were the three musketeers. We were family. I sent Amelia's sperm donor pictures and also sent a letter inviting him to see her; I asked him to be a part of her life and said he did not have to have anything to do with me. He never answered. He didn't even wish her a happy Christmas.

That was it; he was now dead to me.

How could anyone deny this beautiful little baby? You would have to be a heartless coward to not accept responsibility and that is exactly what he is.

I got on with Christmas myself. I made it magical and put up loads of Christmas trees and filled the house with presents. I made a massive Christmas dinner and my dad and his girlfriend came to see me and meet Amelia. It was a lovely day. I was so content.

It was one of the happiest Christmases I have ever had.

CHAPTER 25:

NEW YEAR, NEW START! 2013!

I blissfully started 2013 with my daughters. I felt happy. I knew in a few months I would be packing my house up and moving and I knew that come June/July I would be out of Catterick and away from seeing Amelia's Sperm Donor ever again or having to prove my innocence to a Regiment of soldiers. No more judgements, no more people talking about me in the corridors, no more people laughing at me behind my back, just no more anything. I could enjoy my maternity leave and just wait for my posting order to come through.

I was anxious to find out where I was going to next as I did not want it to be too far from my daughter's boarding school. In January I brought Amelia into the Regiment to do my final bits of clearance and everyone told me how much she looked like my ex. I left him some photos of her in hope that he would see how much she did look like him and that he would now decide to be a dad to her. He did not. Not even a text asking how she was. I figured that's the last time I try with him. He doesn't deserve to be her father. This innocent beautiful little angel had done nothing wrong, she deserved better. I sent one last letter and with that I have never contacted him again.

So now came my next battle. Getting maintenance for Amelia. I contacted CSA not long after she was born but to my amazement by January I was told the father was disputing paternity. I do not know why I was shocked; I should have known he would play delay tactics. Anything to get out of being found out he was a liar on camp after all these months. Right then, I contacted the company back and told them to arrange DNA. By Jan 2013 I had completed Amelia's DNA with the family doctor and now all we had to do was wait for him to do the same. Only he decided to wait until the week before he flew out to Afghanistan late March/April. So by now he had left me thousands in debt, bought nothing on the run up for the birth of our child and now four months in, he still hadn't done the DNA.

Finally though, on the 3rd April 2013 I received the Cellmark certificate back with completion of their decision. It said, combined paternity index = 81,000; this means the results are more than 81,000 times likely that he is the biological father of Amelia than if they were unrelated. It then went on to say probability of paternity = 99.99%. The DNA analysis provides strong evidence that 'unnamed/he' is the biological father of Amelia.

I couldn't believe it; I finally had it in my hands and in black and white. I had waited a year for this result to prove him wrong since the minute I found out I was pregnant. It had been the longest year of my life.

I felt like running around camp and sticking a copy on every door and every lamp post with a massive 'I told you so' header. However, I decided to keep my dignity intact. I did post it on social media though, I was just elated. Finally, I could clear my name.

But the war for maintenance was by no way over yet. He had timed it so well that by the time the result came in he would already be on his way to Afghanistan. I was told whilst he was there on an Operational Tour he did not need to start paying for his child. The Child Support Agency would not support my bid of a claim against him now whilst he was on an operational tour.

It hardly seemed fair. He had got off Scott free for a year without helping towards anything and now it seemed I would have another year to wait until I receive a penny for Amelia. Any decent human being would want to provide for their child, but not him.

I was then told that despite him receiving a lump sum at the end of the tour that this would not be taken into consideration, nor could I have any of the monies owed for Amelia backdated. Little did I know it would be near 2014 before I received my first bit of money for my daughter.

There are no words.

Regardless though, I thoroughly enjoyed my maternity leave. The winter months I spent time bonding with my new baby and come Spring, well I knew I had my four-year bonus coming from the army and this to me meant a holiday with my girls, and also more debt paid off.

Things were good. I had less that £9,000 to go. I was paying bills and getting paid (maternity pay) to just be a mum. This was the life I had dreamed of. I had been clean for over four years now, my house was furnished, my girls were happy and healthy and so was I.

I decided right there and then that 2013 was going to be my best year yet and I would say looking back now, this year was mostly a happy year.

By February I had met and started dating a new man, I knew I didn't want anything serious and I certainly did not want anyone to infringe on my space or time with the girls. He was lovely and at night times I was glad of some male company again to share a glass of wine with.

Abi was back in boarding school after Christmas and Amelia did what babies did best – sleep!

I started to get some confidence back and even started getting back into my fitness regime again. I bought a running pram and come rain or shine I would be out running around the streets of Catterick, desperately trying to regain my pre-baby trim figure. It also helped with my mental health.

I continued to date this man and by March I decided to make a trip to Scotland to see my mum and her husband. I invited him along as I thought what the heck, he seemed nice enough and I thought it's company for the five- to six-hour car journey.

This visit would be a costly mistake.

We arrived in Scotland at my mum's little cottage and at first everything was good but it was whilst I was there I learned this man not only had a wife who was currently away serving in Afghanistan, but he was a well-known fraudster to the police. He had also duped a string of woman out of money and – just like me – they had all been conned by his sob story that he had to leave the army due to cancer.

I stupidly believed his army story as he had an Army ID Card and he also lived in an army quarter but told me this was because the army never made him give up the house whilst recovering from illness. Little did I know it was because it was his wife's home, not his.

I couldn't believe what I was finding out, but yet he was fiercely denying it. His wife was messaging me, other women started messaging me and also a good friend who was out serving with his wife was messaging me.

I knew they all couldn't be wrong.

However, during this time he had convinced my mum that I was wrong and he worked his manipulative charm on her and so this resulted in me and my mum falling out. I headed home; my trip was over.

I had just fallen out with my mother and now I had to make the five- to six-hour drive home with a liar in my car who had caused it all. I should have left him there in Perth to find his own way but me being the soft touch that I am knew he had no money and no way of getting back.

The car journey was horrendous and when I got home I sobbed for hours. I was gutted but more upset that I had fallen out with my mum.

Nevertheless, I carried on regardless.

Over the next few weeks this man continued to scare me and make my life hell. My car was targeted, the tyres were slashed, the paintwork was all keyed and anyone who visited me at my house had the same treatment (car ruined).

When I finally went to the police they knew exactly who I was talking about before I even mentioned his name and – low and behold – I was told he preyed on vulnerable women and he was actually kicked out of the army and never had cancer.

I couldn't believe I had been so stupid.

Once the police contacted him, the trouble stopped and I was free to continue on again.

Those six weeks had just been a really stupid mistake I now knew I just attracted the worst type of men and I really was better off just staying on my own.

In April 2013 I took my girls to Turkey. Just me and my two beauties. We were 'The three musketeers'. It was the happiest holiday of my life.

Amelia was four months old and Abi was ten. Myself and Abi got on so well on holiday and she was such a good helper to me with Amelia, I really would have been lost without her. I had received my four-year bonus with the army and with it I booked this holiday to Turkey at just under a grand, I also paid two thousand off my debt balance and I kept £500 for spending money.

I was getting there. I was now down to owing near £8,000. I had cleared £19,000 in four and a half years. Well, after all I had just been through, I felt like my little family deserved a holiday.

We spent a blissful 11 days in the sunshine and relaxing. It was just what we needed. I didn't even mind the fact I was a lone parent despite having loads of families all around me. I was not bothered, I was just happy and grateful to be here and away from trouble or upset. I have to say though, the Turkish people were absolutely lovely to me, they couldn't do enough for me and were always helping me with the pram or at meal times when I wanted to eat but Amelia was playing grumpy baby.

I couldn't get over how nice everyone was. This was not like Spain, where staff didn't seem to have two minutes for you.

Amelia was as good as gold, she slept most days in the warm Turkish sun, leaving me and Abi time to bond and sunbathe. At night I would watch my girls dance together (well, Abi carrying Amelia around with pride) at the local disco/kids Mini-club and at bed time we would all snuggle up together.

Abi was my best wee pal. Sometimes I forgot I was on holiday with a ten-year-old. She was just like a young adult. We walked all around the island checking out the tourist places and taking in the fresh air and we met some lovely couples who were quite taken with Amelia and how good she was in her pram.

When I look back now, this was one of the best holidays I ever had.

Like everything though, the holiday soon came to an end and on my return home I knew it was time to start packing up the house. No easy task as I had been in it over three and a half years, I had painted it and decorated Amelia's baby room and really made it my own.

This was a completely silly mistake as it was never my house, it was the Army's, and those that have lived in Army quarters will know how strict they are with how the house needs to be when you hand it back.

This was going to take some work.

May 2013 was mainly spent painting, collapsing furniture, boxing things up and taking things to the skip, it was no longer looking like a home; however, I knew it was time to leave this place so I was not sad.

I received my posting order and I knew that come July I was going to be starting work at a new unit in York. I was over the moon as I was literally moving 25 minutes away from Abi's boarding school. I envisaged evening visits with Amelia so I could take Abi out to tea and I knew she would now be home a lot more on weekends. I felt like this was the break I so desperately needed.

Not before another holiday first though. I was determined to have one more trip and when I received a small pay-out for an accident I had previously had in the army I decided right there and then I was going away.

I also took a lovely friend who I had recently made from all the trials and tribulations of the man who had duped me only a few months earlier. She had also been conned by him but out of it came our friendship.

So the beginning of July, complete with my girls we headed to Gran Canaria.

Again, this was another lovely holiday, I love Gran Canaria. The heat was stifling but I loved it. We met some lovely families out there and I have to say between Turkey in April and Gran Canaria in July, they have to be the best, happiest memories on holiday I have ever had. No men allowed, just the girls.

It was a lovely twelve-day break and now it was time to get back and get the hell out of Catterick.

CHAPTER 26: POSTED TO YORK

My posting order was dated 29 Jul 2013. So with that I got moved to York.

The day I finally handed my keys in at Catterick felt amazing. I did not look back, only forward and I was so excited about getting my new home.

My dad still lived in Scarborough so now moving to York meant I was less than an hour away from him. I was now closer to Abi and I really felt happy. I got unpacked and settled into my new four-bedroom army house. It felt huge to me, the gardens were massive, the rooms were pretty big and I just didn't know what to do with all the space. But I was not complaining. It was fantastic.

My friend who I had met during Phase Two training was also on my new camp and it was so nice to see her and spend time with her again. I had two weeks getting settled into my new home but before I knew it, Monday 29th July was soon here and it was time to go back to work after nearly a year off.

I felt I was ready and I knew I could do it.

Childcare for Amelia was expensive but I wasn't the only parent in the world paying through the nose in childcare in order to work. So with that, I started my new job.

After my first day though, I knew I was not suited for this post. A Headquarters was not for me. A building full of Officers. I needed banter, I needed hustle and bustle, I needed people to talk to but this, this was horrendous. Everyone sat in silence and I only spoke if I was spoken to.

I made friends with the other clerk there who also absolutely hated it and I quickly learnt that the last clerk had gone off sick with depression.

This was not like a Regimental post where you knew your job and could be a clerk, here very much any job you got (even if it was nothing you had learnt or had done before) was to be completed.

It was spreadsheets galore, my worst nightmare.

It was also endless days off setting up conference calls and putting out clean crockery for coffee mornings and then washing up. I thought to myself, this is not why I pushed myself through training; I am more than a pot washer. I was basically treated like a skivvy.

I tried my best to settle but could not get used to the routine at all.

Yes, there was still fitness but little to none of the staff would go. Yes, there was still the odd bit of pay to check but very few and far between because in a Headquarters they hire in civilians to do this job.

I couldn't believe it. Why order in a clerk if there was not a more purposeful role for them?

Then there were the endless duties. I managed my duties in Catterick because being in a Regiment, the duties were shared with 15 to 20 clerks a month, meaning you would get plenty of time in between duties, but here, here it was a joke.

There were three clerks and so it meant the three of us took turns, meaning we were on duty every week. It absolutely broke me; not just the fact I was missing precious time with my baby daughter but I was also sat twiddling my thumbs waiting for Officers to finish their work, whilst I was paying through the nose in childcare for the pleasure.

I soon complained and asked to change to weekend duties but even still, this meant paying for later childcare on a Friday so I could lock up, and getting my baby up at 6am on a Monday so I could open up.

They just did not make it easy for single mothers at all.

I tried to settle but I could not get used to the unchallenging basic routine, and to make matters worse, by September 2013 I was very much aware that my Line manager hated me.

I was excluded from a lot of meetings, I was not spoken to when I was allowed to attend and I seemed to get all the shit jobs like cleaning cars, driving Officers here there and everywhere, washing cups and pots after meetings, running errands, etc. All stuff that had nothing to do with being a Clerk.

If I didn't get things, he would make me feel very nervous and so with that and the constant silence in the office my anxiety soon hit the roof.

I dreaded going into work.

On a good note though, during the month of August a new soldier was posted into my department.

Now, after my string of bad luck with men I was not really interested and nor did I pay any attention as he was again a higher rank than me. I said hello when he walked into the shared office he was coming to work in but I never really spoke to him.

On his first day the whole department was told to go out for a meal in order to welcome him into the office and so I did tag along much to my dismay, but upon arrival at the restaurant I found myself sat next to him at the dining table.

I was kind of nervous because I did not want to be there in the first place. I hated being in the company of all these high ranks (it was not me), I was not sure how to behave or if I should speak and to be honest I never really understood Officer-speak. All they spoke about was work.

However, I did start chatting to Jonathan and he seemed to be normal and was just up for getting pissed. This helped me relax a bit but not enough as to not spill my Indian food; yup, I knocked it all over the table.

I was very embarrassed but Jon saw the funny side.

After the meal we all went to the local pub and once again I found myself sat next to him. We spoke for a bit but I knew I didn't have childcare for long so I soon headed home.

The next day at work was his last day of taking over the job before he headed back to his Regiment down South. He wasn't actually posted into this unit for a few weeks yet and was merely popping in to get a feel for what he would be doing. However, back in the office I got a few smiles off him and it was then I thought – *hmmmm, maybe he is okay.*

The next day I received a phone call from him asking me out on a date when he came back to York.

I was shocked he wanted to take me out and also caught in the moment and without thinking I said 'Yes'.

It was only after that I thought, *shit, not another scenario of dating a senior rank.* And more than that, I had just got happy again and promised myself nothing would upset me and my girls again.

Regardless though, something told me to go and so we started texting. Deep down I couldn't wait until he was posted into York fully so we could go on our date and I really hoped it would work out. However, this was me, nothing works out, I told myself.

So now back to September and knowing Jon was nearly fully posted in gave me something to look forward to at work. It made my shit daily routine in that place a little more tolerable because soon I would be exchanging glances over the desk and texting him in secret and it made it all quite exciting to me.

CHAPTER 27: JONATHAN

Our first date was soon here, we had been texting back and forth for weeks and I somehow felt like I already knew him.

However, this did not stop the nerves and so the minute the babysitter arrived, I hit the wine. I was struggling with anxiety at this point because of work and so I felt a shadow of my normal self. I was a nervous wreck. All the days of not being spoken to at work had taken its toll and I had forgotten the bubbly me that I had got back only a few months earlier in Gran Canaria.

I hit the bottle and before I knew it I had drank nearly two bottles of wine and I had also not eaten because we were due to be going for a meal. This was going to be a disaster; I knew I had blown it.

I tried to top up my lipstick before his arrival but I was shaky on my feet, the nerves also made me giggly. So here I was, a drunk giggly idiot with lipstick on my teeth and about to go on my first date. Great, lucky him, I thought.

Nevertheless, he turned up and he was ever the gentleman, he had brought some flowers and the first thing he did was make a fuss of Amelia who was now being watched by the child-minder I had hired. He went in and played with her and it completely melted my heart. I knew he did not have children of his own. He had brought up his ex-wife's child as his own from a young age though, so I already thought what a nice genuine guy he was.

Jon had a couple of drinks to catch up with drunk old me and it wasn't long before the taxi arrived. My heart was pounding the whole way and I was just glad I did have a drink otherwise I would not have been able to contain my nerves at all.

We had a giggle and decided against the meal because by now we were both in a drinking and chatting mood. We went to a couple of bars around York but due to me already being drunk it wasn't long before we needed to get a taxi back.

In the back of the taxi I was as pissed as a fart; I was sweating, I had room-spin, my chest was pounding, my speech was slurred and I just knew I was going to be sick. Luckily we made it back to the house before I was sick but my undignified exit from the taxi was not to go un-noticed, I flopped out of the taxi and rolled onto the grass in my garden.

My room-spin was immense and I was sick.

I was now laid on the grass covered in my own puke and trying to sleep right there in it.

What an impression!!!

Jon was again lovely, he helped me up and put me to bed and sorted the babysitter out. He then slept in the spare room just in case I needed anything or Amelia did.

In the morning I was mortified; I could barely remember what I did but I just knew it wasn't good.

Still, Jon saw the funny side and after he left it wasn't long before we were texting again and arranging our next meet-up. I couldn't believe he wanted to see me again after that disaster but weirdly he did.

The next time we went out I made sure I was not drunk and I made sure we went for a meal. It was lovely and by now I really liked him.

Again he made a fuss of Amelia when he arrived and he seemed really caring and attentive to both our needs. I was starting to trust him enough to let him into my life.

He would listen to my concerns about work and I often told him how much I hated it and it was not me. I told him I was happy that he was coming to work in the same office as me and it had perked my mood at work up. He talked a lot about his career in the army and told me all the qualifications he had gained.

I was impressed.

He told me he was excited for his move up to York and that he was ready to leave his Battalion down South. We talked a lot and we managed to sneak in a few kisses between chatting. When it was his time to go back down South I was sad but I knew it wouldn't be long before we would be working together and I really hoped having him in the office would help me enjoy work a little more as I needed something to take my mind off how much I actually detested my posting to York and the way it was run.

I still to this day have nothing good to say about the place and if any of my clerk friends were to get a posting there I would tell them for their own sanity to turn it down.

Yes, personalities change in a workforce, that's part and parcel of army life but unless the Job specifications for Clerks change there, I can never see it getting better. It was just not my cup of tea at all.

So September came and with that meant Jon's move and our first long weekend away on our own. I had arranged childcare for the weekend and so off to Scarborough we went. The hotel was booked but when the Friday came to go I was full of the cold and I resembled something out of a horror movie; but still I decided to go. It wasn't very often I got full weekends to myself and it wasn't very often I was going away for a romantic weekend, so off we went.

I was nervous but excited.

We walked along the beach hand in hand and I felt happy (complete with snotty tissues).

We chatted and joked and went for fish and chips and both just seemed to be in awe of each other.

We decided to go out for a few drinks that evening but even the simple things like getting ready in a room with a new man made me so nervous. He tried to be nice about it but I had not done this for years.

We went out for a few hours but I was feeling sick and shivery and so we did not stay out long. I couldn't believe it; only me! The first date I was sick from being drunk, the second date I was boring and reserved and now the third date I was a snotty shivery mess who was probably going to spend the first night sharing a double bed with this man snoring, due to the fact my crappy nasal congestion seemed to playing havoc with my life at this precise moment.

I nervously went to bed but – despite my worries – we passionately kissed and I knew he must like me if he was still here given all my nightmare date situations.

He cuddled me until I fell asleep and I knew right there and then I had found a good one, I just needed to stop messing it up.

Easier said than done, this is me, I mess everything up, I thought.

The next morning, we had another lovely day down at the beach but again, I was still full of the cold. However, I was still smiling.

By the end of the weekend I knew we were going to start a relationship; however, keeping it quiet from work would be a whole different ballgame. He hadn't even started yet and here I was once again getting involved with a senior rank. At the time though, I did not care, anything to take my mind off the misery that was work. Things there had got so bad and I really felt at rock bottom every single weekday when my alarm went off. The thought of Jonathan starting gave me a little hope that things would get better at work, but they never did.

They only got worse.

CHAPTER 28: <u>CHALLENGING TIMES</u>

So Jon had started at York and fitted in straight away in the department. I, however, still had not settled.

By now my line manager really hated me and although he tried to not show it in front of the two other clerks, I just knew. He had his two favourites and I was just the black sheep. I got all the crap jobs, I got spoken *at*, not *to*, and still I was being ignored at meetings.

I knew there was an exercise coming up in October and I dreaded it. I had not left Amelia for longer than two nights since birth, so the thought of going away and staying on a camp down south for nearly two weeks filled me with dread. My anxiety was through the roof. Something I do not expect people to understand.

The thing with anxiety is we do not exaggerate our feelings, we cannot help how panicky we feel, and the smallest thing could be a massive challenge in our minds. We cannot help it; it is an illness.

I tried to tell my boss my fears of leaving Amelia but he ridiculed me. I felt like the other clerk was judging me as a soldier but the bottom line was I could not help how I felt and to be honest my only priority was being a mother to Amelia and not leaving her for that length of time. Leaving Amelia under the age of one for that long, to me was the end of the world. I did not care for the opinion of one of the clerks; to me she was a brown-noser, always stuck up the boss's arse and did everything in her power to make me look bad.

The other clerk was lovely and to this day we are still friends. She got me and didn't question my feelings nor did she judge me. She tried to help and so it was decided we would split the exercise and do a week each. My boss, however, would say it was his idea to make himself look good, but really I knew he hated the thought of being stuck at work with me now for an extra week over having the other clerk there.

Regardless though, I planned and organised childcare for one week. The Brigade was busy preparing for this exercise but my mind was very busy going into overdrive with how unhappy I was. I was now dicked for a sporting challenge and I really did not want to do it but I felt I had to in order to get my boss off my case.

The morning of the challenge and I felt horrendous, my ear was killing, my chest was tight and I really couldn't breathe. I tried to tell my boss but he was not interested all he cared about was that I got to the race location on time.

I told him I needed to see a doctor and he simply said, 'Well, you have missed sick parade'. I was fuming. I had not gone sick because I thought it was best to tell them first that I was not well enough to take part in the race. Now he was saying because I missed sick parade, I had no choice but to take part.

I really, *really* hated this man.

He was so manipulative, he made my skin crawl.

I arrived at the location – Castle Howard near York – for the race at eight in the morning; and, low and behold, my race did not start until 3pm, so this meant I had to drive other people about back and forth all day from each leg of their races.

Great, so I now had to sit about just waiting to do my part of the race when I could have gone sick.

I could have screamed.

I sat in the little hire car and sobbed heartfelt tears. How had I let one man reduce me to this? Three o'clock came and I dived into the lake that I had to swim, it was freezing and my chest pain intensified. I could not breathe. I was a very strong swimmer, always had been. The years of training as a child had put me in good stead for life but today I just couldn't move. My mind was telling me to go and just show my boss I was not a nobody, but my body was screaming. With every head-duck into the water, my ear pain felt like I was being stabbed in the side of the head and with every swim stroke, my chest felt on fire.

I was in dire straits.

I was at the back, not just a little bit back but very far behind the others. The safety boat came up to me and asked if I was okay and I explained I was not and that I was sure I had a chest infection and could not breathe but I refused to get on the boat and give my boss the satisfaction of seeing me winched overboard and not finish the bloody race.

I swam on.

I have no idea how I found the strength to complete the 70-acre lake swim, but I did it. At the end, I crawled onto the minibus and cried. I think people thought I was crying because I was last, but I was crying because I was so angry I had been made to complete this challenge whilst sick.

I felt humiliated.

That performance was certainly not me at my best and I am sure he did it on purpose to show everyone how crap I was. I was devastated. Still, despite the humiliation I was still not allowed to leave. I still had to drive everyone about and then hand the hire car in.

Just what I needed. By the end of the day I got home, collected my daughter, and sobbed.

I knew I was still not going to be allowed to go sick the next day as I had been tasked with cleaning all the hire cars that were used for the challenge and taking them all back to the correct department.

It just never ended.

He had scared me that much I felt like I couldn't even tell him I needed to go sick and after trying to tell him before the race, I realised it was not worth the hassle. I was given an unrealistic deadline of twenty minutes to get one car cleaned and handed in and returned back to another camp and then to get back to my camp on time for the team photo.

I was never going to do it in twenty minutes. Everyone knew the car department on camp checked the car over when they got it back and that you had to wash it down and make sure it was spotless. He had set me up for a fail. Once I arrived at the other camp there was another Officer there handing his vehicle in also and he didn't have a lift back to camp so he asked me to wait for him. I couldn't say no as he was an Officer and to me it was disrespectful.

However, on my arrival back to camp my line manager was stood outside waiting for me. Waiting for this Officer was going to prove a massive mistake. As I walked towards the Brigade Headquarters entrance my boss was screaming at me to double (meaning run). I did not. By now I was struggling to breathe with my chest pain and just walking was killing me, so I knew running was out of the question.

Because I did not run, I just angered him even more.

He shouted in front of the Officer I was with and hissed at me, 'Move, you little cunt'.

I met him face to face and he just started storming about and shouting, explaining I had missed the photo and that I was in big trouble with the other Officers because I had let everyone down. He was screaming at me that I would now need to stand and have my face photo-shopped into the photo. He made a show of me and made me stand in the rain alone whilst he took my picture in front of the whole of Headquarters.

(To this day there has never been a team photo of the event released or published in any sporting magazine for our Unit, so I know this was just another way to ridicule me).

After being stood in the rain and humiliated once more, he stormed off. I went into the building and cried. I decided right there and then I had enough and so I went home.

The next morning, I went on sick parade and I did not even bother telling him. It was confirmed I had an ear infection and chest infection and that I needed antibiotics and an inhaler.

I knew it. I knew I was ill but the fear he held over me stopped me from doing the right thing and now my health had suffered more than it needed to. I went back to work after my doctor's visit and told him I was sick but he didn't care. He was still angry from the day before and so I knew from now and until I went on exercise, my life was going to be made hell.

I decided to tell the next boss up from him what was happening, but she sided with him because they were good friends.

He had made out it was all in my head and that I was treated just the same. I knew I was not imagining it and I knew what he was doing.

However, the boss said I could do a five-day, four-night exercise instead of a full week to try and relieve my worries of leaving Amelia. She also granted me a couple of days off before I went. Still, when it came to the exercise all I could think about was the nightmare I was still going to have when I got back.

I cried every single day.

To me, the exercise was an entire joke. There was literally nothing for the clerks to do and I just sat there being ignored every day, making my anxiety even worse. It was a complete and utter waste of money, and at a cost of £100 a day in childcare for me to be away, I was just not earning or gaining anything from being there.

The Officers wanted to go on the piss every night because the Exercise element was mainly in the daytime and so in the evening we were all expected to go out and socialise (something I was not expecting) but I just couldn't afford to go. I thought I was actually going on a proper army exercise where we lived under ponchos and we would be in a field every night. Not this. This, to me, was worse because it just excluded me even more from the team because I did not have the money to join in. Also, part of me felt that I did not want to join in because I didn't trust anyone.

However, after a couple of nights one of the high-up bosses asked me what was wrong and why I wasn't joining in. I decided to tell him. I told him of my fears of going back to work and I told him how much it had cost me in childcare to be here and that I was already repaying debt and just couldn't afford to throw that kind of money away to sit and do nothing. He told me everything at work would get sorted and he also gave me some money to come out that evening but I knew right there and then, come pay day I would pay him back regardless. I had already been humiliated enough. He seemed nice and I trusted him.

I was wrong. Very wrong. Another costly mistake.

He then went back to my boss who had granted me the few days off before I went on exercise and told her I was moaning down there and that I was causing problems.

He asked me, I never went to him.

Now my shit was really gripped, and I was fuming.

I now knew I was in even more trouble when I got back to the unit and now my life at work was going to be made even harder than it already was. I cried so much and so it was decided I would go back a day early from exercise. I was glad. I just wanted to cuddle Amelia and get away from these backstabbing bastard people. They had mentally broken me. I spent a few days at home and then went back to work. As I expected, I was not in for an easy ride.

In fact, it was horrendous.

Between the two bosses back at Brigade, they had come up with a plan to make my bully-boss look good. He denied not letting me go sick, he denied excluding me from things and even showed work emails where he had included me into the conversation. I had to laugh, fair play to him, he was making a good show of making out he was an angel, but I – hand on heart – knew the truth.

Just because he had included me in the odd email proved nothing, there was still umpteen meetings I had not been invited to, there was still the way he spoke to me when he did bother to speak to me, there was still the constant humiliations he seemed content to put me through. There was still the daily nightmare of not knowing what mood he was going to be in and what unrealistic deadline he could give me that day.

And also, during my meeting with my boss they seemed hell-bent on making me out to be a liar, like I specifically went and asked the Officer for money or I asked for a chat. Neither was the case. My boss decided I was not allowed to go skiing in January as a punishment. But really, I was happy. I did not want to go anyway. The thought of leaving Amelia for ten days to two weeks filled me with dread and so despite them thinking they were punishing me, I was actually relieved. It saved me finding the right moment to tell them to stick their poxy ski course up their bloody arse!

However, then came along the situation where I was questioned about my relationship with Jon and so I told them yes, we were now dating but I could not see how this affected my work. The only thing affecting my work was work. Still, I came clean.

To my surprise all they did was move me departments and I actually thought well, this might be good because now I am not on the same floor as the boss who seemed to pick on me daily.

However, once again I was wrong.

Jon could see how miserable I was and despite only being together a few months we decided to go away on our own abroad for a couple of days.

We went to Fuerteventura for three nights, but my God, the clerk who was stuck up the boss's arse didn't half moan about it. Questioning how I could go on holiday without Amelia, but I could not go on a poxy exercise for the full length of time? Well, to me there was a big difference between fourteen nights and three nights and also I was only going because work had made me that low it was in my best interests to get away for a bit.

It was a nice gesture and it perked me up but I knew flying back I was coming home to chaos, and I would be starting in a new department away from Jon.

CHAPTER 29: SERVICE COMPLAINT

So I returned to work once more and I moved to the middle floor department but again I felt isolated. By now the whole camp had been talking about me and my troubles and I felt like I was just being laughed at. Every time I walked into the office, people would stop speaking. I found myself a dog's body once again with no real job. There was no banter, no one of my rank to talk too, no one I really liked and no one I trusted.

I also had heard that the man who offered me money whilst on exercise was now off sick and so I was nervously waiting for his return to see what he had to say to me when he got back, I was fuming with him after dropping me in the shit and changing his story, but who was I? I was only a Junior rank with no value (so it felt anyway). I told myself he was a cold, calculating and conniving man just like the others and I started to wonder if all Officers just went to a specific training school just to learn how to be totally heartless? Still, his absence meant I had some time to get on with things here and I hoped in time the whole sordid exercise experience would be put to bed.

I tried to get on as best as I could but every day was a drag, I went to work miserable, I went home miserable and that was life for months. My line manager was still his charming self, always making me nervous and always giving me tasks he knew I would never be able to complete. If there were any shit jobs to do, you could guarantee they would come my way. If I walked past his office, you could guarantee he would be in there with his sidekick (the other clerk that was up his arse) and I could hear them all the way down the corridor with their comments and gestures.

It was draining the life out of me.

By Christmas I broke. It was killing my relationship between me and Jon because I was constantly miserable and so I decided if the bosses above his head were not going to help me, then the only option was to help myself. I filled in a Service Complaint for bullying and requested a posting out of there. By now I had fallen in love with Jon so between that and uprooting the kids and facing yet again another move meant it had to be bad if I was willingly choosing to leave Jon behind and pack up all my things once more.

It was indeed that bad.

In fact, during those dark months I considered signing off altogether, I considered going back to drugs and admitting it just to get discharged and get out of there but then on the other hand I thought to myself why should I let one horrible, overbearing person put me right back to where I started four years earlier?

I hadn't got this far to lose everything, so my only option was an official complaint.

I typed up my complaint at my desk and submitted it. I got a temporary posting at another unit in York whilst I waited for my proper posting order to come through. After everything, I was so nervous about starting at another unit but everyone at my temporary unit in Fulford were amazing.

I worked in an office with two civilian ladies and they really lifted my mood. They were some of the nicest ladies I have ever worked with and the four months I was there I was a lot happier again. The permanent post loomed over me though and so I was not completely settled. I was living in limbo. My house was half packed up and I was on standby to move. It was still a bit of a worry for me and Jon as I had no idea how far away I would be sent from him.

I had booked Abigail's and Amelia's Christening for December 8th 2013 (exactly a year to the day that Amelia was born). I went about planning that and organising the Church and picking up food to have a small gathering back at my house. It lifted my spirits a little.

I had asked Jonathan to be God father to Amelia because I decided that regardless if we split or not that he was so good with her and I could see how much they loved each other and that he should always be in her life.

My dad and his girlfriend came and my friends arrived with some lovely gifts for the girls. It meant the world to me as I have always been a religious person and very spiritual. My daughters looked like little angels in the dresses I had carefully picked out and I remember this as a happy occasion. I so desperately missed my mother though. We had still not spoken since we fell out earlier in the year over that idiot I had briefly dated. I knew she would be so proud seeing the girls stand at the end of the Church Altar being baptised. Regardless though, it was a lovely day.

My ex-husband's family also attended so they could see Abi Christened and I was actually really happy to see them. We had not spoken in years since I had split with John in 2005. Everyone couldn't believe how grown up Abi looked and how beautiful she was and also people kept commenting on how quick Amelia's first year had gone.

With the Christening over and done with, we spent our first Christmas together that year and Jon took it all in his stride fitting in with my girls, he played games with the girls and fitted toys together for me. We shared the Christmas dinner cooking duties and for the period of the two week Christmas leave we tried to forget about work and the situation I was in. He was always trying to lift my spirits but I was still feeling low, deep down I knew I was moving away from him soon. I was also gutted that I could not attend functions with him because Jon and my nemesis were in the same Mess (a Mess is just a club divided into rank structure, you have to work your way up to get into the Senior Mess).

You are allowed to attend the Mess with your partner if you are a civilian partner or wife/husband but because I was serving and also a Junior Rank and also because of the situation on camp, I could not go with him and so he went to all Christmas functions alone. It caused arguments and I hated the fact I was letting work affect me so much but I couldn't help it. I took everything to heart. I was massively heartbroken that my dream post to York (near Abi and my dad) had ended like this. After the festive period I continued to work in Fulford whilst waiting for my posting order to come through and during this time I had numerous interviews about my service complaint.

I told the people who needed to know my story but when it came down to it, I had no one to represent me because I was on a new camp and no one knew the situation I was in. Whereas he, 'the cause for my complaint', was still sitting pretty amongst his peers back at York and so had lots of support.

It was going to be one hell of a fight.

Amongst all the stress I hadn't realised my period was late and so I rushed to buy a pregnancy test.

It confirmed what I thought – I was three weeks pregnant.

I decided to wait before I told Jon. We were both stressed at that moment and I could never really find the right time. I had so much other things going on that I just put this to the back of my mind. However, less than two weeks later I started bleeding heavily and I just knew I had lost it. I was upset but then at the same time I just told myself it was not the right time and not meant to be. I finally came clean and told Jon but his reaction was not what I was expecting. He decided that rather than support me he was still going to go out with his mate all day on the piss.

This hurt like hell, but then all it did was really confirm to me that this baby was definitely not meant to be. He has since apologised but at a time when I really needed a cuddle and some support, he was not there.

I will remember that for the rest of my life.

By Spring I received my posting order to an Engineer Regiment in Ripon and I was happy. It was still North Yorkshire and so not that far from Abi. I was so happy and lucky that the Army had been sympathetic to my needs and gave me a posting which was still located North of the Country and near Abi's boarding school. I knew it could have been a much worse posting (for instance, down south), but they were fair to me and agreed it was not my fault I was in this situation so they let me stay in the area. I was grateful, *very* grateful, but more than that I was thankful to be getting out of there.

So here I go again, I packed up my house and Jon helped me clean it from top to bottom. It was hard leaving him, as we had spent most nights together and now we were going to have to be a weekend couple. It was so sad but at the same time I was relieved to be getting away from the place that made me think about ending my career and my life once again. I only lasted six months in that God Forsaken unit but my God, I can easily say between that and my drug days, it was well up there with being the worst time of my life.

CHAPTER 30: POSTED TO RIPON

April 2014 and I started at my new Regiment in Ripon. I had moved into a small, three-bedroomed house, again this was Service Families Accommodation.

I was happy, I felt ready to once again face a new challenge.

Abi stayed in boarding school and visited on weekends and so myself and Amelia lived mainly alone from Monday to Friday. Jon would sometimes commute from York to Ripon through the week but the morning and evening traffic from York was horrendous and he hated the drive.

I enrolled Amelia into a nursery and at first it was working but I soon realised with duties and extras it was just not feasible to leave her in a nursery, I needed more flexibility with hours and so I got a childminder for her. Not just any childminder, it happened to be the same childminder I had for Abi way back in Catterick when I first joined. Luckily for me this lady had now moved to Ripon and so as soon as she was free I snapped a space as she had done such a good job with Abi. She had also worked with military families her whole career and understood the crazy timings. It worked in my favour, it was costly but again I would rather work than not work and at that point I still had £5,000 of debt to go. I was getting there though. Regardless of anything, I knew I was doing well.

September 2014 and I had my little sister's (well, not so little anymore) wedding to attend. She had been with her partner well over ten years and I was so happy for them. They were definitely suited and my God, she deserved this happiness. She too had a lot of heartache over the years and although she managed to steer clear of the drink and drugs path, she had been through a lot of emotional upset herself. She had not spoken to our mum for years and had also done a lot on her own. Not without struggles, but here she was about to get married.

She had chosen a lovely small intimate wedding and I actually think it was one of the nicest weddings I have ever been to; however, there was just one thing missing – Jon.

Once again we had fallen out and despite my pleas for him to still come he chose not to. I must have texted a million times on the way up to Glasgow (where the wedding was held), asking him to still make the journey. I told him to just jump on his motorbike and he would make it but he never came. I was heartbroken. Seeing my sister marry meant the world to me. I was giving a speech (her dad, my step-dad, is quite a shy, reserved man), it fell on my shoulders to do this and to be honest I was honoured.

I was, however, nervous and I really wanted Jon there for support.

Nevertheless, I had a lovely day and seeing my sister walk down the aisle with her dad melted my heart. She looked radiant and ever so slightly bashful but I was proud. At the end of the altar they looked so in love and so happy and I couldn't have wished for anything more for her. For love is all you need.

I felt embarrassed Jon had decided against coming.

My sister had forked out a place for him to eat and on a very small budget and here I was, letting her down. I carried on regardless and at the dinner table I gave a faultless speech, if I do say so myself. The bride and groom were laughing and everyone seemed to love it. I got offered a lot of drinks after that speech and I knew I had done myself and my sister proud.

I had felt a little sad my mum was not there, she would have loved to see Jenni wed but we were both still not talking to her and it was just not meant to be. My daughters had a lovely time and although there were less than forty guests in total, it was a wonderful day – small, private and elegant, exactly what she wanted.

I was and always will be proud to call Jenni my sister.

After September came my 30th birthday in Ripon and low and behold once again me and Jon had fallen out.

2014 was shaping up to be a bad year with arguments.

However, my friends stepped in and we organised a trip to Ripon Races to celebrate my 30th. We had a fab day but I can safely say betting is not my forte and I won nothing. We all went back to mine and continued having drinks and a giggle. It was exactly what I needed and they did their best to cheer me up after once again feeling let down by Jon.

Now I can't give him all the blame as I know I am not the easiest person to live with, but Christ I was now starting to think missing important events in my life was just going to be the done thing.

I was fed up of him.

I was still reeling about my sister's wedding and knew no matter how badly we had fallen out that if he wanted me to attend a wedding for one of his family members then I would be there, I just couldn't understand why he could not do the same for me.

This wedding argument was to continue for weeks but now I was going to also sulk about my 30th.

By November we were back on track and getting over yet another blip. On the run up and during the months of summer, I had cracked on with work and I was so happy to be back in a Regiment where there were loads of junior soldiers, and Officers were few and far between. I was relieved to say the least to be away from a Headquarters.

From arrival in April to Christmas 2014 I just cracked on with Regimental duties. I even managed to fit in a nice two-week holiday to Malta with all four of us. Amelia loved the water and splashing around and although the resort was not the best, we made the best of it.

It was still some time away yet before I could afford luxury holidays. Me and Jon weren't used to spending so much time together and admittedly we did argue a bit, some days we clashed, some days him and Abi clashed but regardless, I knew I loved him.

Not everything could go plain sailing. We still had a nice time and it was lovely to just get away.

Back at work, and some days I hated it (I knew my moods played a part in this), and I was over-tired with all the fitness and running around and I also got sick of getting Amelia up at crazy hours just to drop her off at the crack of dawn and just hand her over to someone else to have her for long days.

This was no nine to five job. Amelia had to be dropped off for 7.30am in order for me to start at 8am, and if I was on duty it could be 7 to 8pm before I picked her up. I felt jealous I was missing out on special time with my toddler and I always went to work feeling guilty (I think most parents will understand what I am talking about).

However, some days I loved it at work and the banter was good; I was no way depressed like how I was in York. I went to Belgium for a long weekend with the detachment I was in and I loved it, I had a really good time. I got overly drunk when I was there (what's new?) but I just saw it as me finally letting my hair down and getting rid of some stress from the previous months.

By now me and Jon had been together over a year and with being engaged, I trusted him. He stepped in to help with Amelia so I was not as anxious about leaving her. Amelia now called him 'daddy' and watching the two of them together melted my heart. It was the dad for her I never thought she would have. Regardless of mine and Jon's up and downs, I knew he was a great dad to her.

Things were good but I always felt like something was missing. I knew deep down it was Abi. Amelia could never understand why she just came home on a weekend, I felt rotten that these two sisters were separated. I wanted them to be together so bad but I also knew Abi loved her school.

By October 2014, there were talks of the Squadron I was working in going to the Falkland Islands in September 2015 and this filled me with dread.

Yes, I was no longer as anxious about leaving Amelia for up to three or four nights, but six months plus was just unthinkable. I knew there was no way on God's green earth I would be going. It would kill me. I have absolutely no idea how other military parents do it. I have the utmost respect for mothers and fathers who can go on Tour and just crack on with their job because unfortunately I just could never ever do that.

I don't know if it is because I know how it feels to be left or if it's because I do over-think things and get anxious, but either way when it came to it I just was not mentally strong enough. This thought loomed over me and filled me with dread and I knew my bosses would not let me off just because I did not want to leave my child. I mean, why would they? I signed up and took an Oath of Allegiance to Serve the Country. How the hell was I going to get out of this one? With that, and the constant running around, and also the fact I had missed the promotion board (because my last dickhead of a boss decided to not write me a yearly report as he hated me from the offset, which meant I would have to wait yet another year to maybe be considered for promotion), I realised I had had enough.

I decided by November that I had got what I needed from the Army and now it was my time to sign off. The Army back in 2008/2009 saved me from a life of crime and drugs and debt but now after six months of bullying at my previous unit and the thought of giving up my children for another six months just broke me. I was going to end my service happy and not regretful and so on 11 November 2015 I handed in my notice.

All soldiers have to give a year's notice but also any soldier who has signed off does not have to fulfil Operational Tour requirements.

I was relieved. I felt like a weight had been lifted.

I knew by October 2015 I would be packing up my stuff and moving and this time it would be into my own home.

So with my decision with work and feeling relieved I was now once again getting excited for Christmas.

Jon had proposed and I was over the moon, I think our time apart and all our arguments through summer, September and October, made him realise I was worth so much more than all the upset he was putting me through.

He helped out a lot at Christmas with the preparations and the dinner-making and I was extremely grateful. We all had a lovely Christmas 2014. Jon cooked and I decorated the house with my million trees like I always did. I just loved Christmas. From my dire straits Christmas in 2007, I vowed I would never ever have a Christmas like that again and I can safely say up until now as I write this, every Christmas has been a lovely one spent with my girls and my partner.

We had a giggle and I loved watching the kids open their Christmas presents, it was such a magical time. With Jonathan's proposal and him by my side I knew I now had the stability that I so much craved and that I would never be alone again.

2015 was going to be my year where I could just be me and a mother to my children, where I was left alone and I had no stupid timings or rules to adhere to.

But first I just needed to get there.

CHAPTER 31: 2015 ONE MAD YEAR

So I saw in New Year with Jon; well, actually no I didn't, as we had fallen out and so the end of 2014 I went to bed early and neither Jon nor I were speaking.

Great start, I thought.

It was all about drinking in the house. You see, Jon very much does not like drinking in the house whereas I love a glass of wine or two, but I figured for New Year's Eve we could have a drink together. However, this New Year he was really not up for it as he spent all bloody day making homemade soup that he wanted to try and so he was not up for having a few drinks at all. It ended in an argument and I so did not talk all evening.

We started speaking the next day but still the moment had gone. We always seemed to argue about trivial things. We soon got over it but by now we seemed to be arguing more and more. He seemed to be spending all his time with the Army but I knew this was the way at Christmas; there were always loads of Christmas parties and functions to attend. I still could not attend with him as I knew it would just be an opportunity for everyone from his work to still judge me and also part of me knew if I had come face to face with my horrible ex-boss whilst drunk, then I would most probably end up in jail. I understood why Jon never invited me to places but it did get me down. I still did not feel like a real couple.

In January we went back to work and back to our routine and I now knew in ten months' time I would be free from the army. This lifted my spirits. I started 2015 with just under four grand of debt to go. I had successfully paid off £23,000 since 2009 and I was glad I had done it. I knew by the time I got out the army I would be more or less there.

I knew signing off was the right decision for me and I knew no matter how hard the next few months got that it was only temporary and that things by the end of the year would change. Abi was upset I had chosen to leave the army because this meant that come Christmas 2015, she would need to leave boarding school for good. She had been in since 2010 and loved it.

I told myself I had given her a really good start and an education and opportunity that I would never have been able to give her had I not made the decision to leave Wakefield in the first place.

Abi understood my reasons, she was very grown up for her age and she had seen how tired I got always running around. The Army is definitely a place for the single soldier. I have no idea how families survive the full 22 years together whilst one or both are serving. In fact, I don't think I know a single couple who have stood the test of time. Being on active duty whilst you have a family is one of the hardest challenges to juggle ever. You are dedicated to your family but you also have to remain dedicated to the service. Eventually something has to give and for me there was no question. The Army would always be second and so it had to go.

On an average day a single soldier would roll out of his/her bed around 0730 hrs and get changed into uniform and be on parade for 0800 hrs, then most of them bumbled around and did two hours work before going on a thirty- to sixty-minute break. This brought the day to 1100 hrs and so you only had an hour and a half to work until lunchtime. Lunch was until 1330 hrs and going by the last Regiment I worked in, most knocked off around 1600 hrs.

I am not knocking the lads or lasses on camp by any means, as when they are away doing operational tours or on exercise, they work exceptionally hard; but if you look at a working mother's day in the Army compared to their day you will see why I was always tired.

My alarm would go off for 0615 hrs. I would clean the house, do Amelia's packed lunch, sometimes I would grab a quick cup of tea then I would hit the shower around 0700 hrs. I would quickly get changed then wake Amelia up and dress her half asleep and then bundle her into the car. By 0725 hrs we were on the road to the child-minder's.

I would go through the motions every morning of her screaming and being upset and then I would drive to work. I would usually arrive onto camp for 0750 hrs ready to start the chaotic day where a clerk literally does not get two minutes to themselves. Sometimes we clerks do not even have time for lunch in a Regiment. If I was not on duty I would finish for 1700 hrs and then drive and collect Amelia again. By the time I got home it would be just after 1730 hours and then I would start tea, the constant clean-up and then the bath time routine. Once Amelia was bathed I usually had a mountain of ironing to catch up on and then I had the endless fight of actually getting her to bed. Half the time she did not want to go to bed and so because I missed her, I just went to bed too and so this was my life for months.

I never got a minute to myself. I was always tired. This was just a basic day; this did not include the days we had fitness regimes. On those days I could be in bed for eight o'clock depending on how hard the session was. I was now 31 and I was not getting any younger.

My weekends were not much more chilled either. I spent most weekends making the endless journeys back and forth to boarding school to collect Abi and because I felt bad I was missing so much of them both during the week I spent every weekend cramming in as much as I could with them so that they were happy. It was exhausting for me. So with all that and not actually seeing my children as much as I wanted to, I knew it was my time to let go of the regular army.

I set about making plans for my impending exit from the Army and so later that year I enrolled in some resettlement courses. Resettlement is a package the Army offers soldiers who have done a certain number of years in the Forces, giving them a chance to look at new career options ready for them joining civilian street. It also enables you to look for houses and schools in the area you wish to settle when you leave.

I enjoyed this, I was getting excited about being free. It meant time out of the Regiment where all I had to do was sit in a classroom and concentrate on my future. I started making plans for me and the girls. I planned things I always wanted to do. This included me booking a parachute jump.

I always wanted to do it and so with that I enrolled in a charity jump for Candle Lighters. I chose this charity because it meant a lot to my best friend Kati's family. This charity had given them a lot of support when they had a loss of a child due to cancer. I had never forgiven myself for missing the funeral and I knew this would never replace the time I had missed but it was still my small gesture of giving something back.

The date was booked and on 31st May I would be jumping out of plane. I then booked onto my next course, this time motor biking lessons. Again I had always wanted to learn how to ride a bike and so I could think of nothing better to spend my resettlement grant on other than learning to ride a motorbike.

Jonathan had a motorbike and on the odd occasion we had a kid-free minute we would go out on the open road. I loved it, wind in my hair, my arms wrapped tightly around my partner but still I longed to be the driver and be in control so I booked this course.

Time to make my dreams happen.

This was going to be the year of fulfilling my dreams. By March 2015 I knew Easter was just around the corner and so with that I thought I would love to do one more long weekend stint in Ibiza before I got too old. Yes, I was past the 18 to 30 threshold, but there was still life in this old dog yet, and so in April, I booked us a little getaway.

I was excited. A nice long weekend break just what we needed. We could dance and be happy and watch the sun go down and what made me really happy was that I was in a position now to pay for it myself without bugging Jon for the money. I was well on top of my debt and I just thought well, come the end of the year when I am out of the army, I might not have this luxury.

I felt proud of my little self and I was now on countdown for our holiday.

Come April though, we had once again had a massive argument.

It was so bad we ended up not going on holiday and I was so disappointed that we had argued that badly and so I declared it was over.

I was gutted. I so wanted this year to be our year and now we had this massive fall-out. I had already sorted childcare for that weekend and so rather than sit in the house and cry all weekend I went on a mad Bank Holiday session to Manchester with my good friend Sheree.

It was just what I needed. I really let my hair down and whilst here I switched numbers with someone else. I knew I was not over Jon, but this still made me feel good. I was glad someone was still interested enough to want my number and I felt I did really need this confidence boost. I knew I was drunk because had I have been sober, I don't think I would have given my number out but given the shit circumstances between me and Jon and the fact I found myself now in Manchester and not Ibiza, I just thought 'fuck it'.

I stayed out drinking and dancing with Sheree and I honestly think it was one of the best weekends I've ever had. From start to finish it was just a laugh but then that was Sheree all over, always there and up for a laugh. She got me.

The drive home the next day was horrendous. I was so hung over. I had to hang my head out the bloody window most of the way. I was probably not in the best state to drive looking back, but I had to get back for Amelia.

It was two weeks before me and Jon made up but nevertheless we did, and so with that came talk of our wedding.

We decided to book a venue and we both knew we had really missed each other. I hoped all the petty arguments would stop. I was still upset about Ibiza, I really wanted to go but then at the same time I still had fun away in Manchester with my mate. I just figured Ibiza was not meant to be.

On 19th April I attended a wedding fair at Waterton Park Hotel in Wakefield and I knew this place was the place I was meant to marry. I just loved the lake and the layout and I knew Jon would love it too. He was away with work but still I decided to take the plunge and book.

I knew it had to be a Christmas wedding because there is no one that loves Christmas more than me and when I asked if they had exactly one week before Christmas free, and they confirmed they did, I just knew it was a sign. I reserved the date and told them I would be back with my husband to pay our deposit on my reserve date.

I was so excited. I now just hoped Jon would love it as much as me.

I was so lucky because just under a week later we both went back to view and he did love it too. He was slightly concerned about the cost but I told him we would manage. He wanted to wait until 2016 to marry but I knew it had to be 2015. It would be the magical end of my year after doing all my dream things and then getting out of the army. There was no question about it. 18th December 2015 was my date. It was booked. I was so excited, now I had to plan getting out the army, getting married, moving into my own home and picking a place to settle, finding a new job that would suit me and finding time to complete the things I wanted to do.

It was now definitely shaping up to be my best year yet. I was excited. Every day I went to work happy. There was so much to look forward to and I was so grateful I was here still to live my life.

I felt like I had the world at my feet. I could accomplish anything but first it was time to jump out of that bloody aeroplane!

CHAPTER 32: FULFILLING MY DREAMS

So I arrived at an Airfield near Nottingham ready for my jump.

I didn't feel that nervous. It had always been on my bucket list and so I was more excited to get this done as opposed to feeling nervous.

I turned up nice and early as briefed on the introduction letter and hoped it would be over soon. Much to my dismay, there were loads of budding parachutists all waiting to do the exact same thing. Oh well, I thought. At least it was a nice, sunny, clear day and I can sit outside and watch other people jump.

People were off in groups. They seemed to be calling everyone but me and the longer I watched, the more nervous I became. By now it was early afternoon, I had been there since 0800 hrs, and I was starting to get fed up. For every jump the instructor did, he had to then re-pack the parachute and this took time but it was just not helping my nerves.

At 1500 hrs (seven hours after arrival), I was finally called.

I could see Amelia crying in the car park, wondering where I was going and wondering why she couldn't come. Jon had come along as support, he was probably hoping my parachute didn't open and he got peace for the rest of his life, but unfortunately for him that did not happen!

I hopped on the plane and off up into the sky we went.

It seemed to take ages going up and I slowly started getting more nervous. All the other parachutists were laughing and giggling with excitement but I zoned myself out and tried to mentally prepare myself for what was about to happen. I had not eaten a thing all day due to nerves and I remember feeling starving, but by now I was running off adrenaline.

The door of the plane opened and as I watched the others in front of me fling themselves out, I suddenly started to feel anxious. However, there was no way I was backing out. This jump was categorically going to happen. I had raised over £500 for Charity and could not afford to pay that money myself if I did not jump. Also, I wanted Jon and Amelia to see me achieving something.

With that, I edged myself forward to the plane door.

The cameraman was shouting, 'Smile, and look down for a photo!', but there was no way in hell I was looking down. My eyes were shut and I just waited for my instructor to give me a push.

Off we went.

I was out, I was falling at over 100 miles per hour. I opened my eyes and tried to take everything in but my God, I felt sick. I was not prepared for the amount of spinning we would be doing. Also, prior to the parachute opening my instructor decided to try and adjust the harness mid-flight.

So here I am thousands of feet above the ground and my instructor thinks it will be a good idea to loosen me off a bit.

I honestly have never shit myself more in my entire life.

I could feel myself coming further and further away from his body and I thought, any minute now and he's going to go one loop too far and I'm going to be falling from the sky on my own like a large lanky chunk of meat. My God, I'm going to be crushed like a turnip at the bottom and my daughter is going to witness it all.

I started panicking. I started screaming and my instructor soon stopped. Thank God for that, I thought.

Now it was time to open the parachute. I thought this would be the best feeling but actually when it opened, the force you feel as it drags you back up in the sky made me feel even more sick. Then once opened I hadn't accounted for how much the wind would catch the parachute and send us into a spin. If I thought the spinning was bad without the parachute, then I was in for a surprise because *with* the parachute it was so much worse.

I started retching. The instructor was shouting at me not to be sick. I was trying really hard to hold it in and I was conscious that if I was sick it was all going to fly back and hit him in the face so I had no option but to swallow it. Lovely!

For the rest of the descent down I could not enjoy the scenery or the views, I was just concentrating on not being sick.

We finally came in to land and I did exactly as I was told to ensure a nice safe landing.

The cameraman ran over and asked me to say a few words, I managed to mumble a few thank yous and then the minute the camera was off, I was sick. All the nerves, the not eating, the spinning, the adrenaline, it had all got the better of me.

I cuddled Jon and Amelia. Jon just seemed more interested in getting home, he was bored of waiting and it had been a long day. We started the drive back but I was sick again all over Abi's jacket (it was the first thing I could grab). Yup, this jump really knocked the wind out of me. I think I would have enjoyed it more had I just got it over and done with earlier, like within the first few hours of arrival.

Nevertheless, I did it. On 31st May 2015, I completed my jump. I don't think I will ever do another jump. I have experienced it and have ticked it off my bucket list. Onto my next challenge.

June was here and with that came a trip I had booked to Inverness; my friend Corinne (from childhood) was getting married and had invited me and Jon along. I was so excited. I could show Jon where I was brought up, see Corinne on her finest day and go back home to where my life had all started all those years ago.

We made the long journey up by train but it did not drag, we had a giggle and it was just nice to have some peace from the kids. The scenery on the way up to Inverness is beautiful. I had forgotten how nice Scotland is. It really is breath taking.

On arrival my step-dad had agreed to kindly pick us up and take us to our hotel. I had not seen him for years and I was quite looking forward to it. I also got to introduce him to Jon. They got on so well and this made me happy.

We headed to our hotel. We were both shattered from the journey and we had an early night ready for the wedding.

I was so excited to see Corinne. I had not seen her for years and I knew she had been busy planning and arranging this for months so I knew it was going to be a good day.

It was.

She looked beautiful. I cried when she walked down the aisle. It was so surreal to me to see so many old faces from school. People I had forgotten about but their faces were still implanted into my memories.

It was nice to see how people had grown up and turned out. It was a lovely day and I am so glad I had the honour of seeing my longest-standing friend in the world marry the love of her life. She looked blissfully radiant and I was so happy for her. We did not stay at the evening reception for that long, we were both shattered from work and then the travelling and we also faced the long journey back to Ripon the next morning, so after a few hours at the night do, we said our goodbyes and left.

I was so glad I went to the wedding though. It was lovely to see everyone and I felt happy. Now time to get home and carry on planning for my own Christmas wedding, I thought.

We had less than six months to go and were just paying bits off monthly. I was used to always paying large chunks out a month anyway, as the previous years I had always been clearing debt. I was now down to £3,000 debt and it was manageable (I told myself the average UK household has double this) and so I concentrated more on my wedding. Probably the wrong thing to do, but I was a girl with dreams. Plus, after seeing Corinne's beautiful wedding and venue I was more determined than ever to achieve this.

Jon was paying the venue off in instalments and I was paying for all the little things. I had found my dress and was paying this off, I had booked our honeymoon to Egypt for New Year and was paying this off, and I was buying decorations, favours, balloons, name cards, table glamour, aisle decorations, the chair covers, the sashes, the bridesmaid's money and so on, so I was definitely contributing.

Jon's mum used to be work in a florist shop and kindly agreed to do my flowers and so at least I knew I didn't have this expense! I was starting to realize I could pull this off.

We decided not to get fancy cars as this just added to the cost and I decided it was best if I just stayed at the venue the night before with my daughters and bridesmaids. It would be easier if I was there because then all we had to do was get Jon to the venue on time.

We continued paying things off monthly but at the same time my exit day from the army was looming and we were house hunting like mad. We had agreed to move to Barnsley, South Yorkshire. We chose this area because I wanted to be near to Wakefield where my friends are but I did not want to live in Wakefield itself due to the trouble I had, years earlier. We also chose Barnsley because it is a twenty- to thirty-minute drive to Jon's mum's from there.

So with that in mind, we started looking at houses, and by July we had found one.

On arrival I didn't like it. I thought the estate looked too council-like and I sat in the car arguing with Jon about if we should bother to view it or not. We went in and viewed it though, and despite some crazy wallpaper, it turned out to be our perfect house. The couple who owned the house were lovely and were in a rush to move due to ill health within the family.

The garden was beautiful and big and I pictured myself sat in the sun watching my children play. It was a three bedroomed semi-detached house. Nothing fancy, but to me it was perfect.

This would be our home.

My first place to settle in years. It was to be my everything. We put in an offer and it was accepted and with that the ball started rolling and the countdown for leaving the army had really begun.

My life was about to start and I was moving once more but this time was hopefully to be my last time. I was soon to be free and I was soon to own my very own home.

A dream come true.

CHAPTER 33:
LEAVING THE ARMY, MOVING ON

Summer leave was looming and I was so looking forward to some time off. It meant I could crack on with packing up my house and hunting for wedding things. In hindsight I probably should have spent more time on job hunting and sorting my C.V but I didn't. I didn't care for that; I was too excited. I was about to move into my very own home and for the first time in years have stability.

I couldn't for the life of me remember when I felt stable. It was all I longed for. Yes, I always had a home with the army and it was cheap rent but at the end of the day when the army is over what was I going to be left with? This house to me meant more than anything. I was so grateful to Jon for agreeing to buy, without him I could never have done it. I didn't have savings. Christ, I just spent the past six years paying off debt but this had stood me in good stead on my credit report. I had been paying debt on time for years now and so my report was looking good enough to be accepted for a mortgage. That had to count for something, right?

We put the mortgage into our joint names and I was so excited. We owned a house together. It was to be the start of our life together. The girls were excited although I don't really think Amelia understood what was going on. Abi was happy with the location because it was twenty minutes from her dad although she still felt sad about leaving boarding school. I did feel immensely guilty and still to this day do. If I could have continued with the army a bit longer then I would have for her sake, but after everything at York my heart was just no longer in it. She understood, but I knew it was going to be tough for her at Christmas when the time came to leave.

My heart strings were always pulled as to what do for the best. On one hand I had my beautiful grown-up teenage daughter who needed me to stay in the army so she could stay in a school she loved but then on the other hand I had my toddler who was just getting passed from pillar to post whilst I moved around with work and then worked stupidly long hours. I also craved the stability and time for me. I wanted so much to just have more time to be a mum. I also knew I could not face a long time away from my kids in the Falkland Islands and so I decided this decision I made was for the best.

I just now needed to spend the rest of my life making it up to Abi. If I had thousands of pounds, I would have given them so she could have remained in the school that made her so happy, but the fact was, I didn't. I wasn't and never will be rich. I know this. Some people aspire to make millions, my aspirations consist of stability, not just with a home but a stable mind and all I really want to be is a mother and left in peace. This is when I am happiest.

The thought of being months away from my dream meant that nearly every day in 2015 I was smiling. I no longer cared what people in the army thought of me, I had put the horrors of York behind me and realised the only time I can be me is when I am not letting other people judge me and bring me down. I had a new found energy for life and this summer was just a happy one. I had too many things to look forward to. My daughters were going to be back together by the end of the year, I was going to be in my own house and married, I had new job prospects to try (part time of course, I was no way leaving the army to spend more time with my children to then go and work full time elsewhere), my honeymoon to go on, Christmas as husband and wife, a new life to make, and boy oh boy, I just couldn't wait to get started.

Finally, all my struggles were coming to an end and I knew despite everything with the army I had made the correct decision in the first place with joining. It gave me the opportunity to fix myself. I am not saying the army is the easy option if you are in a mess because by God, leaving Abi and making the initial decision to join was by no means easy, however I look back now and I am so glad I did it. It gave me the chance to fix myself and get to where I am today.

August was soon here and I knew this was the month me and Jon would get our house keys. I also knew I could not finish at the Regiment until September because that is all the leave I had to use. So although I was actually classed as still in the Regular army until November, I could finish in September due to leave days saved and resettlement days saved. September was good enough for me but I knew it was going to be hard getting my house keys in August and not actually getting to live in it for another month after. I would do it though.

I still carried on packing up my house. I had lived in this home from April 2014 and in the year and a bit I had lived here I seemed to have once again accumulated so much junk. I tell you, moving is a good thing because it gives you the opportunity to have a good clear-out. My house was starting to look empty but I didn't care, it was all for a good reason. Good things come to those who wait, I told myself.

On Monday 17th August 2015, the Regiment returned to work after a three-week summer leave period. I knew my time with the Regiment was coming to a close and I was excited. I also knew on Friday 21st August we were getting our house keys. The sale was complete. I was over the moon and had agreed to give up my army quarter on the Thursday. I figured I would just commute for the last month in work as there was no point paying rent for an empty house and I was so excited to live in my own home, I just could not wait.

However, on the Wednesday at our normal Detachment meeting my Line Manager surprised me and presented me with a leaving gift and told me I could finish that day. I was over the moon. I could not get out of the office quick enough. I had spent sixteen months with this Regiment and although it was not bad (they had treated me well) and I enjoyed most of it, I was now so looking forward to the next chapter of my life and my freedom. I said my goodbyes to my work mates, packed up my desk and drove out of camp.

Just like that, my time in the army was done. I was free.

I joined the reserves 18th August 2008 which lead to the Regulars and now seven years on almost to the day, my time was done. I had achieved what I needed to. I was drug-free and had been for well over six years; I had bought a house, paid back most of my debts, had found a lifelong partner and had so much to look forward to. For the first time ever, I was proud of myself.

I had done it.

I handed the keys in for my last ever army quarter not with ease though, of course I would be charged on my final move. They were not happy with the walls downstairs or Abi's room and were now billing me for a re-paint. I couldn't believe it, I had managed all these years not getting billed and then on my final ever march out I got billed £297, I have since disputed it and got it down to £100 but still, I was not impressed, I knew that house was spotless when I left it because as I have always stated I have always been a clean and tidy person.

This bill just reiterated the fact how much I was doing the right thing. No more bloody rules, I could live in my own house the way I wanted to live and more than that I could paint the walls. I no longer had to stare at magnolia – something all army houses are painted top to bottom in. It's plain and boring and after years of living like that it starts to get tiresome.

I got in my cramped car full of last minute packing and I hit the road, collecting Amelia on the way from her child-minder's. Saying goodbye to my child-minder was sad, she had not only been there for me and Abi initially but she had now been there for me and Amelia. She will always be a lady I class as way up there in my estimations. She has dedicated her life to not just her children but other people's children and had followed her own husband around in the forces for years. I don't think she knows how lovely she is and what a wonderful job she does but to this day I will always remember how she helped me out not just once but twice. We said goodbye and promised to keep in touch and I hoped to see her at my wedding at Christmas; and so with that, myself and Amelia were on the road to Barnsley, South Yorkshire.

It was only Wednesday and we were not getting our keys until Friday so we stayed in a hotel close by. I relaxed with my daughter and felt happy. I was free. I was going to carry on being paid with the army right up until 11th November so I was not yet worrying about money. Things were good.

All I had to do now was sit back and relax and wait for Friday to arrive along with Jon who was still currently at work.

Our new life was about to begin.

CHAPTER 34:

SETTLING INTO CIVILIAN LIFE

Moving in day was finally here. Abi was with me now as it was boarding school summer holidays and so the three of us waited patiently in our new garden whilst Jon went and collected the keys.

I was so excited; it was like all my Christmases had come at once. My girls were together for now (soon to be permanent) and I was about to walk into my very own home for the first time. The sun was shining, the birds were tweeting and it was just a beautiful happy day.

The mortgage company we signed with had left us a new house-gift in our greenhouse – essentials like toilet roll, kitchen roll, cups, tea and coffee, washing up liquid, cleaning fluids and so on, and I thought this was a really nice touch. I sat in the garden going through it and then my new neighbour came around with a bottle of fizz and some plastic glasses.

I knew right there and then I was going to love living here (I was right. I am now eight months into living in my new home and I still categorically believe I have made the best decision for me and my girls).

Jon soon arrived with the keys and we were all like storms in a teacup whizzing around the house and checking everything out. I loved it (well apart from the wallpaper, but that could be changed I told myself). I have to say that the couple we bought it from left it in a brilliant condition, everything was spotless and they had made the effort to go around the house and leave little notes on everything to explain how it worked. They had also left some lovely wine glasses and this made me smile. It was the little things.

We soon started unpacking and making it our own. My little Amelia was running around all happy and was over the moon she had a big garden to play in and Abi was busy putting her stamp on her bedroom. Things were good. We were all happy. I don't think Jon wanted to go back to work, he very much had big plans for the house and his mind was always thinking of ways to improve it. Being an electronics engineer, he kept coming up with new ideas and inventions and I knew that he was excited about our future just as much as I was.

After a few weeks of living in our home my attentions soon turned back to the wedding planning and I actually think Jon was glad he was living on camp because he soon got sick of me harping on about it. I didn't care though; it was going to be a magical day just as I had always dreamed of. Buying things and planning made me happy, it gave me a focus and with no work at the minute I was enjoying putting my heart and soul into the preparations.

I ordered the flower girls' dresses and my invites were out. I had started the table plans and was getting excited about my upcoming hen do. My friend Rachel had taken over organising it because in July I had felt really let down by my close friend's lack of interest. In fact, I was so let down it had caused me and my best friend Kati to fall out. She was pregnant, which I understood, and so I picked Leeds as the Hen do venue because it was very close to her work and local for her, I had planned just to arrive at the hotel, all have a nice swim and spa and chill on the Friday then go out for a meal then all I really wanted on the Saturday was a photo with my best friend and my sister and the group. I had never had a professional photo-shoot with either my best friend or sister and so it meant the world to me. I then had planned to go to a few pubs, nothing fancy, but Kati had not asked for the time off work on the Saturday and now had decided not to bother staying for the weekend as there was no point. She said she would come after work on the Saturday but this upset me loads because the main thing I wanted her there for was the photos. I spat my dummy out and lost it. I had tried to make it so she was included through her pregnancy and now she wasn't really coming and missing the best bits so I was crushed. I felt like cancelling my hen do altogether but then Rachel piped up she would organise it for me.

I had met Rachel way back in 2009 during training and then our paths crossed again in 2013 when I got posted to York as she worked on the same camp. We have always remained friends and she is definitely a good lass to have in your life. She is loud and proud and lives every day to her fullest. With her now organising my hen do I knew it was going to be a fun weekend. I still felt sad I had fallen out with Kati but I just left her to it. I did not want to continue arguing throughout her pregnancy and so for the first time ever we lost touch. It was a hard time but I was not going to feel guilty for the rest of my life just because I wanted my best friend there alongside me at my hen do.

Life goes on.

Things with me and Jon were good and I knew at Christmas I would be taking his surname. Amelia had now been calling him 'dad' for years. She met him when she was six months old; I decided that I wanted her to take his name too. Her sperm donor had never bothered turning up to register her and so with just me on the birth certificate I knew I had full parental rights and did not need to ask his permission. I mean, why would I? He had been out of my life since March 2012 and never once asked how my pregnancy was going or asked how she was when born. To me, he had no rights at all and so I applied to change her name by deed-poll.

On 15 September 2015 it was confirmed and I had the certificate to confirm my little Amelia was now a Prendergast. Jon was over the moon. He loved our little girl with all his heart and I knew that if we ever split he would always step up and be a dad to her just as he has done with his other daughter. This was 100% the right decision, I just could not wait until my name was also the same.

I filed for her new passport and went about changing her name in all the legal places. It was a lot easier than I thought and to me Amelia now had a dad on paper. It was the best outcome I could have wished for. On the other hand, at this time I did get some upsetting news on another outcome.

I had received confirmation of the outcome of my service complaint which I had put in just over a year before with the army. It stated that there was not enough evidence on either part.

I was devastated.

I knew my Career Managers had taken it seriously as they had moved me out of that Unit and got me somewhere local to serve to please me. I guess that was a main positive that came from it but still I had clung onto the hope that my claim for compensation would pull through. I went through a lot of heartache and not only that, it effected my career. I was a year behind in terms of promotion and this really dented my pride. I chose to just crack on, I knew something had to give and I told myself it was time to draw a line under the whole experience.

It was time to let go.

I was not going to let this bring me down, I was in a happy place. This little blip was not going to set me back and so as per normal I picked myself up and got on with life.

Friday 23rd October 15 was soon here and so the fun filled weekend Rachel had planned was about to commence. I wasn't sure if my liver could take it but I knew whatever was in store it was going to be fun and I wasn't wrong. Between Rachel and my friends, they had thought of everything. I felt special. Rachel had even made little itineraries of the weekend's events, she really put a lot of effort in and I loved her for it.

First stop, we all checked into the hotel and cracked open the drinks. We had adjoining rooms complete with four in each room. My close friends Athina and Clare could not come on the Friday and so were just coming on the Saturday for the day. So for now it was just the eight of us but it was still enough people to cause chaos. I was over the moon my sister had made the trip from Perth to Leeds for the event and felt really happy. Jon had Amelia for the weekend and so I could have a stress free worry free weekend to myself with my girls.

So our weekend had kicked off and it wasn't long before I realised we were off to a photo studio for the night to have professional photos done of our group. I was so excited, it was a real first for me and I couldn't wait to have a photo, not only as a group but with my sister. I was sad Kati, Clare and Athina were not there but I told myself had they wanted to be, they would have been, and so I got on with it.

We arrived at Pylon studios hosted by a man named Charlie and all I can say is 'wow'. What a great guy, we all felt relaxed and at home and he really went out of his way to make us all feel special. I loved it and once the wine was flowing, I had such a laugh.

We all took turns getting our hair and make-up done and all took turns to have individual photos over a number of different backdrops. We then moved on to group photos and I was smiling from ear to ear. I had piled on the weight since leaving the army in August but this was because I was happy, I was content and I no longer cared what size I was. Cross Country running was far from my mind now. My husband-to-be loved me and so did my daughters and friends. It was time to start loving myself as I am.

Us girls had a cracking evening and I think if I remember correctly it was gone 11pm before we left the studio. Armed with full faces of make-up and fancy hair do's, we headed to Leeds City Centre and continued the party. We drank, danced, messed around and had a laugh. In the early hours of the morning we headed back to the hotel and by now I was feeling worse for wear. I had drunk way too much. The over-excitement had got the better of me. I went to bed feeling drunk and I woke up at the crack of dawn sweating alcohol.

I knew I was going to be sick. My God, I was dying. I had no idea how I was going to last another day on the piss in Leeds. I woke everyone in the hotel room up with the sound of me being sick and for the next few hours I was the brunt of the jokes and called the lightweight of the group.

I had to laugh. I took it all in my stride and by lunchtime that day I was ready to get back on it.

My sister though, well I think I had actually killed her! She was so hung-over, bless her. She had never really been out on a big do with me and she had never really been out with a bunch of squaddie girls. I think I just opened her eyes to the life of an army bird . . . The only way to get through was to live for the weekends.

She was suffering, bless her, and I felt really guilty but part of me did see the funny side. So next on our itinerary was a cocktail-making private master-class complete with nibbles. Well, this was exciting. I had no idea how to pour a beer correctly without it frothing over the sides, so cocktail-making was surely going to be a giggle.

We all lined up at the bar and got stuck in. We were taught how to make a number of cocktails and of course all the while playing team-spirited drinking games. It was good fun and for now I was managing to stomach more alcohol. The nibbles we had on arrival really did help a little. It was such a fun couple of hours and once again Rachel had done me proud.

We all had some lunch at the bar we made cocktails in and then after that it was back to the hotel for some pre-party games. I had no idea what to expect but when a little naked butler walked through the door with only a small apron covering his modesty I couldn't help but laugh, I now knew I was in for a grilling. I panicked in case they had plans to tie him to me all night but lucky for me and lucky for him, they didn't. Instead, I was questioned on things about Jon and things we had been through. I got quite a lot wrong. It made me laugh and everyone else. They had got to know some of my deepest, darkest secrets and I was cringing at myself. For every question I got wrong, I had to drink a shot and so I knew this night was going to end up with me yet again steaming.

After all our games we said goodbye to our butler and all headed to our next venue. I knew later we were off to Oktoberfest as we were all dressed as Bavarian girls. We looked ace. However, before that, Athina had arranged a private Karaoke bar. We had a private booth so we could all sing to our hearts' content and without people laughing at us. Now I am the worst singer in the world, so a private booth to let off some steam was great.

I loved the whole experience and I soon discovered I was not the only one who couldn't sing. However, I was by far the worst. Still, it was all taken in good spirits.

We then hit the dance floor at another part of the pub and it wasn't long before the hen party dare cards came out. What a laugh. Soon I was getting random piggy backs off strangers, trying to blag free drinks at the bar, pinching random people's bums, removing items of clothing and downing random drinks. This day was just crazy and we weren't finished yet. Now it was time to hit the Oktoberfest bar and join in with all the crazy festivities. It was ram packed and I couldn't move. People kept bumping into me and I couldn't for the life of me get to the bar.

After an hour I decided to go to a bar across the street. When it's too busy I start to get really anxious and the small cramped space around me was making me feel claustrophobic. It was of no fault of any of the girls, it was just me and my crazy self.

I left most of them in there and I was actually glad to have half an hour to sit in a bar and gather myself and my thoughts.

It wasn't long before the others joined me and we soon continued dancing away as a group. I had had an epic weekend. They all really did make it a memorable one for me and I loved it.

The morning came and it was time to say goodbye to Jenni and see her off back to Scotland and it was time to say goodbye to the girls. I was so happy and so grateful to them all. I really had a wicked time but like everything, all good things must come to an end and with that I headed home and went back to my hubby-to-be and little Amelia. They had had a nice weekend too and so all was good.

Halloween was around the corner in our new house and so I went about planning the girls' costumes. I had put my name down to abseil off the Sheffield Hallam University building for the charity 'The British Red Cross' and so before any trick-or-treating could be completed, I had this to achieve first.

I wasn't about to do this challenge alone though. This time I roped Jon and Sheree in and between the three of us we raised over £400. With it being Halloween, we all got dressed up. Jon went as a can of spam, I was a skeleton and Sheree was a devil. Jon flew down the wall. Heights didn't bother him at all. All I could do was stand and watch, knowing me and Sheree were going to take the plunge next.

I didn't realise how scared I was going to be until I got up there. I think I was more scared at this than I was with the parachute jump; this was because with the parachute jump I was tied to an instructor and could shut my eyes. This time, I had to keep my eyes open and had to launch myself of the side of a building.

The initial dropping over the edge was the worst and the minute I was over I just wanted to get down as fast as possible. I started pushing myself as quick as I could down the side of the building. I was conscious Sheree was still above me and also nervous but if I stopped to wait and looked down I knew I would panic and so I had no choice but to fly down as quickly as I could.

My heart was racing the whole way down but with my partner and my daughter watching there was no way I was not doing it. I got to the bottom and felt proud, another thing I had achieved.

Sheree also completed the abseil too with no hiccups and I was so pleased we had achieved this together. Now time to hit the bar and take Amelia to a Halloween party. I think we deserved a drink after that.

Amelia loved the Halloween party in the pub and when we arrived home our neighbours were also having a Halloween party and so we joined them for an hour or two. We did not stay that long as we were tired from the day's events but it was nice to know our neighbours liked us enough to invite us around.

During November I had by now started my motor biking lessons that I had booked earlier in the year as part of my resettlement. The first few lessons and I really enjoyed it but then when my instructor changed I started to not enjoy it as much. I was disheartened and felt like he was not a great instructor. All he did was make me feel nervous. I was put on a bigger bike than what I was ready for and it really shattered my confidence.

On one lesson after really struggling I decided to call it a day and that I would try again after the wedding because I just wasn't getting it at that precise moment. I told myself straight after the wedding and some time out I would be back on it. I had already achieved a lot this year, I knew one day I would also eventually achieve this and get my license but now it was just not the right time.

Now my final pay cheque with the regular army was looming and to be honest, since August I had made no real effort to find another job. I was too busy enjoying my freedom, being a mummy, planning my wedding, settling into my own home, settling Amelia into pre-school, having fun on my hen do, doing things I always wanted to do but never got time to (like start writing my book), that work and earning money had not crossed my mind.

Shit the bed, I did not know where to start and I needed to think fast.

I had provisionally thought about the Army Reserves earlier in the year but I didn't think I was actually going to do it, but now it seemed like a good option. Working in the reserves part-time and still having time to be a mummy seemed like a good choice to me and so I agreed to go back to where it all started in 2008 for me. I made an arrangement with my boss to go and help at 299 Parachute Engineer Squadron in Wakefield. It was agreed that I would work three days a week and to me this sounded perfect.

I had not left the army completely after all.

CHAPTER 35: BACK TO REALITY

So off I went back to the reserves, the unit that gave me a stepping stone back into the army way back in 2008 and had they not accepted me I would never have got the chance to sort my life out and get clean. Maybe now it was time to give something back.

However, after the first few weeks I was miserable. I told myself to give it time but I was plonked in a little office on my own and it made me feel really anxious. I was worried some of the people who were still there from all those years ago would remember me as I was and not see me as I am now. There was still faces there that I recognised and they recognised me, I knew that some (not all) were wary of me just as I was of them. I tried my best to get on but I really couldn't settle. I don't settle as quickly as others do at new places. I think all my moves have a massive part to play in this. I stay quiet and remain nervous for weeks until I work people out.

There was no one really for me to talk too. No flutter of soldiers that would come in and out of my office. No banter, no life and to top it off I had been put me in a department that helped recruit soldiers. Something that requires a specific skill-set and at that precise moment my heart was not set on learning this role.

At the time I felt I was hardly the correct person to try out a recruitment role. Still, I tried, but I hated it. I told myself to continue until Christmas leave and maybe after the wedding I would feel different and so for now I persevered.

I can't fault the Officers and the staff that do work there, they are all lovely and they all did their best to accommodate me. I think they knew I was not enjoying it at that time because most of the time they left me alone. With Christmas once again looming it gave me something to look forward to and for once this would be the first Christmas where I could attend Jon's Christmas function as his girlfriend/wife to be. Not a Junior soldier.

By now all the people that upset me at York had left (this is because most soldiers get posted after a certain period of time, this included the person I felt picked on me, he was gone) and I felt ready to step foot back onto that camp and for once just try and have a good time. I felt happy and proud to be Jon's partner. We had a laugh at the table and although it was not the best function I had ever been too I was glad I went. I released some demons I had carried with me all these years since leaving in 2013.

Jon won a sound speaker system at the raffle and I was just happy with the free wine on the table. We had a lovely night and I met a lovely couple whilst there. I was so glad I finally got to attend a function with my partner.

So now it was time for my Christmas function at my own work and my God, I didn't half get drunk. I was extremely nervous because I was so unsettled there at that time and so the more time went on, the more I drank and with that comes 'nightmare Vikki', the Vikki that cannot hold her tongue; and so as the early hours of the evening started, so did I. Completely wrong time and place and it did lead to a big fall-out.

We had more or less started to calm down when more people started to get involved and I felt rather than stay and argue, I should go home (probably my first sensible decision I had ever made when drunk).

Some of the things that were said to me really upset me and I realised some of it was probably deserved as I should never have gotten that rowdy on a night out; however, I felt even angrier now. I was now raging in fact, I was fuming. Now I was so angry and knew there was nothing I could do about it so I burst into tears. Yes, I shouldn't have got drunk in the first place but I certainly did not appreciate or deserve some of the scathing remarks.

I decided to go home. The next day I had no intentions what so ever of going into work. In fact, the following week I decided to clear out my desk. I was already miserable and unsettled there and now staying was just going to be ten times harder.

My boss came and spoke to me and said I should still try and attend the next Squadron Christmas function. At that precise moment, there was no way in hell I was going but when the date came, Saturday 12th December, I decided to go and show face.

I was not going to be pushed out of this unit because of a daft drunken argument because let's face it, we have all done it.

Armed with my hubby-to-be, we went for a few hours. Turned out that we had a nice time and it went better than I thought. I did not speak to the other people I had initially fallen out with and nor did they speak to me, it wasn't the time or place and I think we had both learned from the last experience. Discretion being the better part of valour, I avoided those I had an altercation with earlier.

I just got on with my night and met some nice couples who were sat at my table. I won £30 in a money raffle and I enjoyed the food. Myself and Jon decided not to stay that long and so just before ten, we decided that I had done well by showing my face and also by not getting drunk this time, and so with that we left.

Upon leaving, my boss came and wished us well for our wedding and said he hoped to see me back next year. He was pleasant and so I started to think maybe I had been too hasty, after all it was me that started the bloody argument; however, it did not change the fact I really did not enjoy the work in general and I was not settled.

For now though, it was going to have to be something I thought about after our wedding. At this precise moment all I could think was I that was going to be 'Mrs Prendergast' in six days.

I was by now so excited. Abi was getting out of boarding school on Thursday 17th December (the day before the wedding) and so it seemed all my dreams were coming true at once. I was ecstatic. I did everyone's head in, harping on about the wedding and my constant Facebook updates. Our honeymoon to Egypt had been cancelled due to trouble overseas and terror alerts and so we had now booked to go back to Inverness and also the Lake District. To be honest, I didn't care where we went, I just wanted some time on our own together with no fighting and no glitches but yup, this was me, nothing was that simple.

There were also two very important people still missing from my life, my mum and Kati. I had written to Kati a week before now, apologising for my upset over the hen do and I told her I had a space open for her at the top table. By now I knew her second son was newly born only a few weeks prior, so I was not sure if she would answer, let alone come, but the least I could do was invite her. I congratulated her in my e-mail on the birth of her son and told her it would make my day to see her again. There was nothing more I could do. I had made the first move to fix things.

That week though, I received a card in the post. I knew straight away it was my mum's writing. I was shaking opening it. By now we had not spoken since March 2013 and I had no idea what was going to be inside. I procrastinated for ages about opening it but curiosity got the better of me and I opened it.

My mum had wished me and my husband-to-be luck and love and with that I burst into tears. It was a starting point to forming a relationship with my mother again. I didn't know what to do at first and was very confused but I decided to message her and thank her for her card and warm wishes. I didn't feel it would be right to now invite her to the wedding just days before the big day. It would have made me nervous and also it would have been a little awkward between my sister and mum as they had not spoken for years.

However, I knew my mum would be thinking of me and I knew after the wedding we could start rebuilding our mother daughter relationship.

I was happy.

CHAPTER 36: MR & MRS PRENDERGAST

So the big day was here, Friday 18th December 2015. To say I was excited would be a massive understatement. I hardly slept the night before with nerves and excitement. I was hoping all my plans and efforts would come together nicely.

I stayed in a room at the venue with my two daughters, my sister and another bridesmaid. We shared champers and soon other guests who were travelling to Wakefield had started to arrive. I was so excited to see them. I knew come morning, the next time I would see them would be walking down the aisle.

I was nearly there. I was nearly at my happy ending. The fairy-tale for me was about to come true.

Yes, Jon and I had our ups and downs but today was our day and I knew I loved him. This was us, here and now ready to make a lifelong commitment and new start. I was over the moon, we had come through a lot since August 2013 and despite everything we were still together showing the world we were about to unite as one. I was no longer going to be the lone warrior always struggling.

I decided Abigail was to give me away. She was thirteen now and had been with me through thick and thin. She is a beautiful girl and I am so proud to show her off. My step dad (Jenni's dad) unfortunately could not make it due to work but I didn't mind, I understood.

My real dad Steve made it though. I didn't think he would due to ill health; he had been in hospital all the way to the lead-up to the wedding. He was on crutches but he made it, that's all that mattered. He arrived complete with his girlfriend and my brother Matthew. I also invited Matthew's mum, after all she did take me in all those years ago back in 2001. She had always been lovely to me throughout the years and I was happy to see her again.

My aunty (mum's sister) also arrived with her husband and I was so glad to see her too. Good friends I had made from the Army camps attended. I was so grateful people were making the effort to see my special day come alive.

Us girls started getting ready and as the hairdresser and make-up artist I arrived I could feel my nerves creeping up. Little Amelia was excited, she had a lovely white and blue flower-girl's dress, her friend Erin (Jon's brother's daughter) was also a flower girl and she soon arrived to keep Amelia company.

Jon's mum came to my room and wished me luck. She thanked me for making him happy but really all I could think was it should be me thanking her for giving me her son and making me happy. My sister and Athina looked beautiful in their bridesmaids' dresses and soon Sheree arrived (my other bridesmaid) and now it all started to feel real. I had offered for Jon's daughter to be bridesmaid and originally she said yes but as it got closer to the time she declined due to her own personal circumstances.

However, her son, Jon's grandson, was still to be included and he had the very important job of carrying the rings on a small white pillow. I knew he would make a great ring bearer. He is the most handsome little boy you have ever seen. So I had my three beautiful bridesmaids, my two flower girls and my Abi as Maid of Honour. The ceremony was due to start at mid-day and before I knew it, it was time.

I left my hotel room and headed down the stairs towards the ceremony room. My heart was pounding. We all lined up ready to walk down the aisle. I watched the others go through one by one and by now I wasn't just scared, I was terrified. I held Abi's hand so tight I nearly ripped it off. She was my rock and I couldn't imagine walking down the aisle with anyone else. She knew I was scared but kept telling me I was okay. I could not have done it without her. I was so nervous. All eyes on me. My worst nightmare. It's like an anxiety attack waiting to happen.

I walked through the doors and I clapped eyes straight away on Jon and with that I blocked everyone else out and walked straight to him (I didn't know at the time because of adrenaline but everyone told me I practically ran down the aisle). I was just so happy he had turned up. I was so happy our moment was here.

The ceremony room looked beautiful with blue and silver chair covers and birdcages just as I imagined. I caught sight of my dad and he looked so proud. I caught sight of Jon's daughter and she never even raised a smile. Still, I ignored it.

It was probably just me.

The Vows went better than I thought and I managed to get my words out clearly and concisely without a hiccup.

My beautiful Abi gave a reading and my God, she didn't half do me proud. Right there, right at that very moment, I wanted time to stop and take in the beauty I had created. It was perfect.

After a short thirty-minute ceremony we were pronounced 'Mr and Mrs Prendergast' and my heart burst with pride. Everyone was clapping (well, mostly everyone, there was one person who was not).

It was a nice time for a few pretend photos signing the registrar book. I loved it. We had done it.

We walked back up the aisle as man and wife and I can honestly say, less for the birth of my children, I have never felt so happy. It was time to let the celebrations begin. We had done it. I was elated.

The wedding co-ordinator handed us a glass of champers and I think I was so hot in that room after standing in my layered ivory gown that I downed it. I was soon given another one and so now the wine was definitely flowing.

We posed for family and friends' photographs overlooking the lake. My guests were given nibbles and drinks whilst we waited to be called forward for the wedding breakfast. I tried to make my way around talking to everyone but by God, it's hard. I only had 65 adult guests so God only knows how other brides with large guest figures manage.

Still, I made the best of it. I think every time I stopped at a table I was handed a glass of wine and I knew this could only end badly but I was getting carried away with the moment. Jon looked happy. This made me happy.

We all went for our wedding breakfast but first the preliminaries before food, time for the speeches. I was nervous and excited for these. I knew my sister was doing one for me and I knew Abi also wanted to do one for me. I knew Jon had not prepared anything and was doing it 'off the cuff' but that's just him all over but I was nervous for his best man's speech. We had had a fall out years before and so I had no idea what to expect.

Abi and my sister's speech blew me away. I laughed and cried and laughed some more and everyone seemed to enjoy it. Jon's was a typical groom's speech. He thanked everyone and handed out the gifts. He made a couple of jokes and then handed over to the best man. I sat in panic mode waiting for him to start and soon I realised this was not going to be about his friendship with Jon or anything to do about the wedding. This was going to be the moment he stands up and talks about his army career and himself for what seemed like hours. It just went on and on and on. At one point he even made reference to how Jon met his ex-wife. I was starting to get fed up but carried on smiling.

I looked around the room and could see everyone was getting fed up too. Everyone was starving. It was now gone 3pm and all people wanted to do was eat. He had been talking for a good fifteen to twenty minutes when Jon's daughter suddenly decided to take it upon herself to walk out.

Now, I am no wedding co coordinator but to me this was extremely rude (I was since told she needed the toilet; madness, no adult walks out of a speech for a toilet break, well so I thought anyway, I could be wrong). Yes, I got the speech was long and boring and trust me, I was not enjoying it either but we were all adults so surely she could have done the right thing and waited just like everyone else had too.

And so that was the start of her bad behaviour for the rest of the day, well in my opinion anyway. I had no idea why she was being a little awkward.

Yes, when Jon and I initially met we had our ups and downs and on my part sometimes I had not handled it well and ranted on Facebook but I had not done this for nearly two years now and had previously apologised for it, could she still be annoyed with me about that? I had hoped not as I had tried so hard to include her in the wedding, what with asking her to be bridesmaid and so on.

Granted, she came and spoke to me and Jon at the top table after we had eaten and was pleasant enough but something wasn't right. I was still a bit upset she had decided not to be bridesmaid despite me trying my hardest to include her but I respected her wishes; however, I was a bit annoyed she had decided to keep the bridesmaid money we had given her to buy a dress. I was also a bit upset she had not bothered bringing Amelia (her now step-sister) a birthday gift. Her birthday was two weeks prior to the wedding and I never even got a message wishing Amelia a Happy Birthday; but still, I let it go. I knew she knew it was Amelia's birthday because I was sat next to Jon when he texted her and told her. So there was that, but then there was the fact she had not even bothered bringing a wedding card. Yes, I got that maybe she did not like me but not giving a 'Congratulations Card' for your own dad's wedding seemed odd to me.

I felt a bit sorry for him because all he ever seemed to do was help her out. Still, I ignored it. I had also ignored the fact that she arrived to the wedding fully dressed in black. A short black dress. I didn't think people came to weddings dressed in short black dresses. I thought this was really rude and I don't know if it was because I was used to the Army way of all functions had to be a sensible below-the-knee dress that I found her choice quite disrespectful.

I also really thought between that and with the money we had given her she could have bought a nice new dress, not overly expensive, but at least more formal. Still, I got on with my day and just ignored her miserable looking face. Yes, because every time I looked at her she was not smiling. I knew she had gone through some recent problems of her own but I at least thought she could raise a bloody smile for her own dad's wedding, I mean come on, it's not that hard. If I went to my dad's wedding, and no matter how much I disliked his partner, I would still turn up with a card and a smile on my face at the very least.

But today, there was to be none of that.

The evening reception soon came around and by now I was really hoping Kati would turn up. She never arrived at the day do, so I had my hopes on her arriving at the night do.

She did not come.

One of my bridesmaids texted her to ask if she was coming, and she had chosen against it. That's a real shame, I thought. I really thought she would come; still, I did not let it ruin my day. The evening events started and a few more people started to arrive, my auntie who had been at the day do made me laugh as she decided to go home and change her outfit ready for the evening do. Well, at least someone was making the effort, I thought.

My cousin (my auntie's daughter) arrived with her partner and I hadn't seen her in years so it was nice to have a catch up. Everyone seemed to be having a good time. But I can honestly say from about 8pm onwards I cannot remember a thing. The wine had got the better of me.

I had arranged for one of the guests to dress up as Santa for the kids and bring them a small present and so when it came to the first dance Jon was nowhere to be seen. The DJ was calling him and calling him but he seemed to take forever. Turns out he was helping Santa get ready. Finally, he arrived and I had a drunken wobble of a dance to a mash-up version of *With or Without You* and *Sweet Child of Mine*. We heard it earlier in the year whilst in Dublin and instantly fell in love with it. I knew right then this was going to be our wedding dance song. Our wedding rings were also bought in Dublin because we wanted something a bit different plus we both absolutely loved Dublin. So there was a little bit of that with us on the dance floor.

There was, however, someone missing from the dance floor cheering us on.

Yes, yet again his daughter had stormed off. By now I really believed she was not happy for us, either that or she really did hate me to do this. All the signs were right there. Jon went off to get her after the dance and I was later told it was because her life was falling apart and we looked so happy. I thought to myself, what? That could not wait? At that precise moment you needed to make our first dance as a married couple about you!

I was livid but regardless I did not say anything.

What I did need to do was go and have five minutes alone in my bridal suite and re-touch up my make-up and just take a time out; however, on getting there Jon had already let his daughter in for a lie down with her son.

So now here I was in my own bridal suite sat on a chair in complete silence whilst his daughter, who had done nothing but appear to be awkward all day, now laid down on our bridal suite bed.

To me this was the last straw. What I didn't get was why she was not in her own room? She is a grown adult and had known for nine months her dad was getting married so why hadn't she booked her own bedroom, it's not like she didn't have the money, Christ we had given her some for a dress that she clearly didn't use, she had not bothered buying anything for Amelia's Christmas or birthday so I knew she must have some money.

Oh, but wait it gets better, she hadn't even bothered asking her boss for the following day off work so now she needed to find a way home.

So after sitting in my room for a good twenty minutes with her just laid staring at me on my bed I thought fuck this and went and got Jon. I told him I had had enough and so he asked her to leave. He said he had let her in there because her son wasn't feeling well. Well, I understand that but again what I didn't understand was why did she have to use the bridal suite? There were loads of people there (family) with rooms, why pick ours? It seemed to me she was hell bent on spoiling my magical day that I had worked so hard making perfect. She soon left and with that I had had enough. I was annoyed and so I went to bed.

My head was spinning and I was now really disheartened. I left Jon at the evening reception and he made his apologies for me but now I just wanted to be alone. I couldn't believe how heartless she had been towards us. Jon came in later and went to bed. We both just went to sleep. We were knackered.

In the morning we did not talk about what had happened with his daughter instead we decided to open cards and gifts. The last thing I wanted was to start arguing the day after our lovely wedding but by breakfast I knew something wasn't right and my gut feeling told me this charade with his daughter was not going to go away.

I was right. I started going over the last few months in my head with his daughter. She had been messaging me fine, I even told Jon to send her flowers when she was going through an upsetting period. We had spoken about Christmas gifts and I told her I had personally gone out my way to buy her a nice girly gift as I knew her dad would not have time. I asked what her son would like for Christmas and I had been asking her all the way on the run-up to the wedding how she was, so now I could just not get my head around her behaviour.

My family and friends had noticed it too and it seemed the only person who had not was Jon. I knew I wasn't imagining what just happened. Still, now was not the time or place to bring it up and just like that the wedding was over and it was time to pack up all our lovely things and head home as husband and wife. I was excited now for Christmas, we had plenty of booze in that we were given as wedding gifts so I knew I did not need to buy any of that. The house already had a few trees up and all my gifts to the kids were wrapped and ready. I had the joys of a Christmas savings club to thank for that. Christmas day soon came around again and we all had a lovely morning.

Amelia was now three and really understood what Christmas was about and so seeing how excited she was on Christmas morning made my day. Abi was also delighted with her gifts and so all in all we had a lovely morning. It had been agreed Abi would spend the afternoon with her dad so I had booked me, Jon and Amelia into a local restaurant for our Christmas dinner. However, on the way there I stupidly logged into Facebook and saw Jon's daughter's post with a mountain, and I mean mountain, of presents for her son.

By now I had seen red.

So not only had she not bought Amelia anything for her birthday, she now hadn't bought her anything for Christmas and what made it worse, I had cut Amelia's gifts back in order to buy her a bloody decent and expensive present.

She had not yet apologised for her behaviour at the wedding and now the spoilt brat just seemed to be rubbing my face in it.

I was livid.

I can safely say I did not enjoy Christmas dinner. I could have been eating with Royalty and it would not have made a difference, I was livid and Jon knew it. I didn't say anything that day because after all it was Christmas, but by Boxing Day I had erupted.

Myself and Jon went to the pub on our own and I let rip about every niggling thing he had let his daughter get away with. In fact, I was so angry I used some foul language to describe her recent behaviour. I have no idea to this day why I let her bother me so much, but at that precise moment and over the wedding, she had.

This resulted in a massive argument, and before I knew it, Jon was gone.

So that was it.

I had been married days before the arguments started.

I knew then it was never going to change, and it was over. I got that he would stick up for his daughter, I will always get that but I will never get what he did next. Everything I had said to Jon in our private conversation in that pub was relayed straight back to her, word for word and so now to this day she uses this against me. She uses what I said after the wedding as an excuse for her behaviour at the wedding.

The whole charade was now a massive deal and none of us would budge on sorting it.

CHAPTER 37:

<u>HAPPY FUCKING NEW YEAR</u>

I spent New Year's Eve alone and crying. I was meant to be in a lovely hotel in Inverness celebrated Hogmanay the Scottish way with my husband of two weeks but nope, once again I was in tears and being ignored because I dared to question his daughter's behaviour.

I must have cried all night. Poor Amelia was with me and she had no idea why mummy was sobbing. I felt guilty for that. My heart was being ripped out. Why could nothing just ever go right for me? The next morning my lovely friend Sheree told me she would come up for the day and night so I wasn't alone and so that evening whilst I had company I decided to get unbelievably drunk.

Yes, it definitely didn't help but at that time I thought it did. All the wedding champagne we had been given as gifts got drank. For that moment it cheered me up a bit. I just could not believe I had been married less than two weeks and I was seeing in my first New Year alone. The previous New Year we spent it not speaking too and I started to really think I had made a massive mistake by marrying him. Deep down though I was gutted that she had come this far between us.

My heart was broken.

During the day of the 1st January I had agreed to Face-time my mum for the first time in near three years. I was a little nervous but when she rang I realised how much I had missed her. She listened and we talked everything over. I told her about my wedding and I told her I missed her. I told her about Abi and Amelia and I told her how I met Jon and that I had got out the army.

I was so glad I had my mum back in my life.

She had now been sober years and I was happy for her. She was generally a lot happier in life and I was so glad she was a lot better. We never really spoke of our fallout, we just both knew it was not worth it and now it was just time to start getting our mother-daughter relationship back on track. At that precise moment in my life she could not have come back to me at a better time.

My mum is a wise woman with many life experiences and despite her upsetting years in the past she was a lady you would always want to have on your side. I was proud of her for what she had come through and it was only now after experiencing my horrendous addiction battle and mental health dark dog plague that I really fully understood how well she had done.

Yes, she had a drink problem but I could not hold that against her, I had learnt over the years it was an illness and an illness she had defeated. She had done it and I now know it would have been the hardest obstacle she had overcome. Not everyone with alcohol addiction comes through it but she did. The past is the past, I was not just happy to have my mum back in my future. If anyone was going to understand my lows now, it would be my mum. We chatted for ages and I found myself smiling again. After the phone call I could not wait to tell Sheree I got my mum back. I was excited. We ordered a takeaway as I realised I had not eaten in days with all the stress of the fallout and we carried on chatting and drinking champers into the small hours.

Mine and Jon's fallout continued for weeks but we decided to try and put it behind us and move on. He came home and although we actually never spoke of a resolve between me and his daughter we tried to get on for the sake of our marriage. Again I knew this would not be the end of the argument and that it would creep up later. I was still angry that after everything she had done at the wedding – or not done, should I say – was then followed by an initial text from her of abuse. We had text-argued for a few days over the period me and Jon were not speaking but I decided enough was enough and I blocked her.

To me she was not and will never be sorry for ruining my dream. It was time to try and concentrate on my marriage. I was upset I would never get the honeymoon period back or our first New Year's Eve as man and wife but I told myself life goes on.

We had received some money from the wedding and so I decided to book a cheap and cheerful holiday to Portugal for February. I decided it would do as all some good as a family. I then decided on going to Dublin for Valentine's weekend straight after Portugal, I knew it would be good because it was where we always had a really good time and it was 'our place'. We loved it there.

We had arranged to go with another couple and so just like that we had something to look forward to again. I asked my mum if she would like to come to the house and watch the kids after we got back from Portugal so that me and Jon could have our trip to Dublin on our own. I thought it would be really good for my mum to see the girls; after all, it was nearly three years since she had last seen them. She was overjoyed with the offer and could not wait until February to see my home and her granddaughters. I was happy too that I had made this step forward. I never thought I would see the day where my mum was back in our life, but here we were, getting on.

Things were definitely on the up.

First things first though, it was time to go back to work. I had taken a month off from my Army unit over the Christmas period and I felt like this was enough time to get over the fallout I had previously had. So I went back, after all I was not lazy and just because I was married did not mean I solely wanted to rely on my husband, I had always looked after myself and provided for my girls and I was not prepared to lose my independence. I liked earning a bit of my own money and so with my tail between my legs, I went back.

I told myself it would not be that bad as I was only working three days a week. I got back into a routine with taking the girls to school and slowly life started to go back to normal. It took me a whilst to settle back into work but by the end of January I was starting to enjoy it and I was glad I made the decision to go back. My boss and I cleared the air and I finally admitted I had bi-polar disorder (Cyclothymia, a mood disorder that falls under the Bi Polar Family) and that I had been diagnosed in 2011/12 with this mental illness, I explained with that and feeling nervous and getting too drunk, this was the reason for my outburst at the first Christmas function. I told him it would not happen again and that I would never drink like that again on Social functions.

We all started to move forward and for that period I felt happy, I was enjoying my job again and I really started to settle at long last.

I took part in my first Cross Country Challenge in over a year and I walked away with a Trophy. I felt happy. Part of me had missed the fitness side of the army life. It had always helped with my mental health. I started to think this year was not going to be as bad after all. Abi was now living at home full time after leaving boarding school at Christmas and although she missed her old school dreadfully she had settled in her new high school and made some lovely friends. As per normal, she had done me proud and taken the change in her stride.

Before I knew it, it was 1st February 2016 and it was my husband's birthday. I had bought him a nice designer watch and gave it to him a couple of days before because unfortunately he was working down south on his actual birthday, however that did not stop me sending him a really exciting message. There was no better day than today to tell him I was three weeks pregnant.

We were expecting.

This was to be Jon's first biological child. He was over the moon. I really felt like this baby had been sent to us a gift to help us secure our relationship. I was over the moon, although I never saw myself with three kids, ever. Nevertheless, I was happy. It was time to knock the wine on the head and stay healthy. It would do me a world of good having an alcohol-free year. Just what I needed after a month of partying in December and then my massive blow out on New Year's Day.

I was ready.

However, I soon realised our holiday to Portugal was less than a week away and Dublin was two weeks away.

Oh well, a sober holiday for me.

Off we went to Portugal as a family and although the island was quiet and the weather was not great, we had a nice time. We met other lovely couples out there and the break did us good.

I admittedly had the odd glass of wine with meals but was in no way drinking heavily. The all-inclusive food was nice. I loved all the fresh fish and salad and for me it was just nice not to cook, clean and run around after the kids. We had a little apartment and Abi did not feel safe sleeping in the living room on a pull out bed so Jon took this pleasure for the eight days. I felt for him a little bit but I did not want Abi to feel unsafe.

Towards the end of the holiday I was starting to get nervous about seeing my mum again. I knew on the day we got home she was coming to see the kids. We were due to fly home from here 11th Feb and then fly to Dublin on 12th Feb. We got home, dumped our bags off and I rushed off to the train station to collect my mum.

It was lovely seeing her again and I knew she was happy to be back in our lives too. She was so happy to see her grandchildren and my living room resembled Christmas morning with all the gifts she had brought for them. I knew she had missed them and knew they would all be absolutely fine for the weekend without Jon and me. We chatted until quite late and then just like that in the early hours of the morning I was heading back to the airport.

I was excited. Dublin is by far one of my most favourite cities in the world but not only that, I had great memories here with Jon. I knew we would have a lovely weekend. On the Friday morning when we arrived we had a full day to ourselves exploring prior to the other couple arriving and so we went back to all the bars where we had fun memories in.

It was just what we needed. The other couple soon arrived and together we all had a giggle. I surprisingly didn't feel that left out that they were all able to get pissed because right then at that moment I was just happy without drink.

On Saturday we went to a waxwork museum and again had a laugh and again Jon and I went off exploring. If I had the money I would pack up my house and move there but as most people who have been to Dublin will know, it is very expensive. Valentine's Day I was given a lovely engraved heart with the words 'Our first Valentine's as Mr & Mrs Prendergast 2016'. I loved it. I was brought chocolates in bed and I felt happy. We had another nice day and then flew home. My mum was shattered when I got back, she had forgotten how hard it was running around with a toddler but she had enjoyed every minute of it.

Monday morning, she headed off to the train station and I promised I would come up and see her with the kids at Easter.

We had a lot of lost time to make up for.

CHAPTER 38: EASTER 2016

The next few weeks I really got my head around work with my unit and was now understanding what my job fully entailed on the recruitment side. I had been given a more prominent role than just helping with recruiting (I was now inputting pay and doing clerk stuff, things that were familiar to me and jobs that I enjoyed). I was happy. I started to feel like I was fitting in.

It seems to take me ages to settle anywhere but after a few months I am generally okay. I had also started to panic about the new baby coming and money. I still had nearly two grand debt to go, what with the wedding and my last remaining months on my loan, and to me I really want nothing more than to be completely debt free for when the baby arrives.

I decided to try another job alongside the army work. I had been given an opportunity doing care work and gave it a go. I completed the training and was really enjoying it. I thought I would do really well with it but on my first day out doing care visits I was sick. I was not sure if this was because of morning sickness of the pregnancy or if it was because of the delightful smells that come with working in care. Unfortunately, this wasn't for me. It was not because I did not care for the elderly but at that time it was just too much for me and so that was that. I would just stick to the good old trusty army work. I had tried.

I was meant to be going away skiing with the army for two weeks but again, due to pregnancy, I could not go. I was actually relieved. Once again I did not feel ready to leave Amelia for that length of time. Still to this day, I think the most I have left her in one go is four days. Two weeks would kill me. I know it sounds daft to most people but I really am a home bird now. Even more so since getting my own house. I have moved so many times and now just being at home with my children and feeling secure and content means more to me than travelling the world – for now, anyway.

A lot of people question me as to why I hate leaving my children and I do not expect people to understand. Without my children I would not be here and to me the only thing I can give them back is my time. I know after this pregnancy I may struggle with the army as again things will crop up where I am needed to go away. I can only imagine I am going to be worse with not wanting to leave home with three kids but I can only cross that bridge when I come to it. For now, I was happy just working in the office and coming to my own home every night. It's the simple things.

I did however, book a small trip for Easter for us all to go and see my mum. I had promised her in February that I would make the effort and come and see her and I felt I needed to do this. I was nervous because as stated at the beginning of the book me and her husband never got on and then since the fall out in 2013 I was dubious about it all but that did not deter me from going. A lot had changed since not only my childhood but since 2013.

I thought what with Jon on my side everything would be okay. I wanted my mum to get to know Jon and I wanted her husband to meet him. We were due to travel by train on Good Friday to Perth. It would be perfect, a nice Easter weekend in Scotland building a relationship with my mum again. She has a beautiful little cottage and I knew Abi loved it and I could not wait to see Amelia running around her massive beautiful garden complete with wildlife and a river. It was to be idyllic.

Myself and Jon had tickets to see Dynamo in Leeds the day before we were due to go to Scotland and I was so excited. I loved his work and every time I watched him on TV I was mesmerised. It was going to be a great night, or so I thought.

However, on the Wednesday evening Jon was out on a works do. Whilst out it occurred to me that he had told me he was going to be working in Bristol that night and that we could not go and watch Dynamo on this Wednesday night for this reason. I texted and asked him why he told me he was working away if in fact he was actually at his unit out on the piss? I could not remember him telling me he was no longer going away so I questioned it. Silly mistake on my part texting him when out.

Low and behold, it started a massive argument that just seemed to get bigger and bigger. And so that was it. That was us back to not speaking. Combined with my anger and his responses, (which were followed by apologies on his part) the damage was now done.

On the Thursday he asked me if we were still going to see Dynamo and then to Scotland the following day? I was still fuming with him, I did not want to be anywhere near him let alone stuck at my mum's with him, so despite me really wanting to see the magician I decided not to go, and I also made the decision to go to Scotland without him. I had had enough of the arguments and last thing I wanted was for us to go away arguing.

Yes, maybe I shouldn't have asked the question. Maybe it was the wrong thing to do but was I really meant to tip-toe around for the rest of my life too scared to ask a question? The evening came and went and I sat looking at our tickets. I was crushed.

Yes, he started apologising but I was too upset with his reaction in the first place, to me I did not deserve that and the damage had already been done. I was also by far not over the fall out with his daughter at Christmas and so still reeling with that and now this new argument, I went to Scotland on the Friday alone. It was hard because I really needed him to be with me. I was already nervous for going back to my mum's after all these years and now with Jon not there I felt like once again I looked like a failure. I was ashamed. I went for the kids' sake and to be honest it was a lovely weekend spending time with my mum again. Even her husband was lovely to me. He is very much set in his ways now (well, he always was really, but now with age it was even more apparent), but then tell me an older man who isn't? I had to try and respect the way they lived and for the first time in years we got on. It was not as bad as I thought. The Scottish country air was just what I needed and Amelia loved it.

Abi was in her element because my mum is make-up and cosmetics mad, she has more make-up than a beauty store, so Abi spent hours looking at it all and trying it all out. My mum made us all feel welcome and I was so happy to be there. At one point in my life I thought I had lost her for good. I will always feel sad when I think back to our fall-out in 2013, we missed so many years but I guess it's in the past and right now I am just happy I have my mum back in my future. I love her so much regardless of anything that has happened. I just sometimes wish I could have just been a better daughter. I wish I helped her more through her dark days but instead I judged her and got angry with her. I guess through her worst periods I was only young myself and not living with her and having a mountain of my own issues meant I could not be in two places at once. If I could take back anything it would be that. However, here she was, stronger than ever and now she was trying to help me get through my fall-out with Jon.

Jon continued to text-argue with me whilst I was away and it was quite stressful. Before I knew it, his daughter had been brought back up and despite knowing this had not been properly put to bed I just knew I could not be arsed with it anymore. It had been months walking on eggshells on this subject. I tried to get on with my weekend.

On the Saturday I met my sister Jenni (who also lives in Perth and I also met my step dad). We took Amelia to an indoor play area and we all had a catch up. It was nice to see them again. I had not seen my step dad for a long time and I wanted to thank him for our wedding money he had sent. It was that which paid for our holiday to Portugal. I could not face telling him Jon and I had fallen out so I simply said he was working. Jenni knew though. We said our goodbyes and I headed back to my mum's cottage for the rest of the weekend. I spent time with mum chatting and catching up over things I had missed. Come Monday though, I was ready to go home. As much as it was lovely seeing her again, my head was still reeling with the argument with Jon and I needed my own space to get sorted.

I tried to get back to normal as best as I could. I attended Amelia's parents evening alone. She was doing really well and I was proud of her. Abi was starting to have regular fall-outs with girls at school but I think this is just teenage girls and their age. She is still going through this stage now and I am hoping it passes.

It was soon April and me and Jon were still arguing. The stress and upset was unbearable. I was lost and confused. That, complete with pregnancy hormones, made me feel really low. I could not believe this was happening again, another pregnancy on my own. By now we had argued so much about his daughter. The more he tried to defend what she did, the angrier I got. It was a vicious circle. He sent me a text showing she did try to apologise to me but I never got it because I had blocked her. In the text I read the words 'I never liked you'. I was livid. My whole body was shaking in anger. All I could think was, how is this an apology?

Yes, she had apologised for not bringing a card to the wedding but she lied her way out of not knowing it was Amelia's birthday. She said she never knew. I had to laugh because I was sat next to Jon on the day he texted her and told her. Then came the comment of not ever liking me. Well, that's done it for good now with me, because to me if you never liked someone you certainly do not accept expensive gifts from them, nor do you take advice from them when feeling low nor do you agree to be bridesmaid in the first place, nor do you take money for our wedding fund, in fact if I didn't like someone I don't think I would pretend to be their friend in the first place. Had this girl no morals at all?

Trying to tell this to Jon though was another story. He could and still to this day cannot see it. We argued and argued and argued until one day I just had enough and blocked him. I had my unborn baby to look after and all this stress was not helping me. My health was going downhill with crying. My hair was falling out, I had stress ulcers all over the top of my legs, I was exhausted from not eating and sleeping, my mind was once again fragile and I really was feeling broken, he had broken me down. He had tried to tell me everything with his daughter was in my mind but I knew this was just a sick decoy to try get me to change my mind about her. Something I will never do now. I will never have anything to do with her again. She had caused me so much upset from my wedding day and the fallout from it and now hearing she had never liked me was the last straw. I felt used. I decided right there and then she would never be part of my life or children's life ever again.

Yes, I would never have stopped Jon seeing her, it's his daughter but by God, I didn't have to have anything to do with her. Let's face it, she had seen Amelia like three times since I had got with Jon, she had missed her birthdays and Christmases and made no effort. Why should I let her let me and my kids down anymore? With the decision made, I started getting on.

My first scan was booked for 7th April. I needed to see the baby on the screen. I needed to see he/she was okay. I had gone through weeks of heart-ache, I was now really worried so much so that I had paid for a private scan. My friends Clare and Athina came with me and the minute I saw the little heartbeat flickering on the screen, I knew I had to pull myself together once again for my kids. The emotional turmoil I was putting myself through was not good for anyone. I emailed Jon a picture of the baby and he seemed happy.

The days started getting easier and I continued to work and juggle the school run and my mummy duties. I knew I had my NHS scan coming up soon and I invited Jon along despite my anger with him. After all, this was his baby too. We met outside the hospital and we never spoke a word to each other. The whole appointment was spent in the same atmosphere. We were silent in the waiting room. We were silent walking to and from the waiting room. In fact, it could not have been anymore awkward if we tried. The whole situation was heart-breaking. If it wasn't for Amelia being sat there then it would have just been an awful silence. This was the first time he had seen Amelia in weeks. Mainly because he had been away but always because I wanted to make sure he was not going to take her to see his other daughter against my will. I agreed Amelia could spend that night with him after the appointment and to be honest I was glad of the night's rest.

I went home, collected Abi from school and decided to take her out, just me and her. She had seen my upset for the past few weeks and it was not fair. It was time to both smile again. We went to the cinema and watched a comedy and we both laughed again. It felt really good. I started to really think I was better off on my own and the very next day I started making plans for the house and this baby's arrival. By now I was 15 weeks and after seeing the baby at the scan and knowing he was okay I felt I was now safe to start buying baby things. I started buying the essentials, a steriliser, bottles, few bits of clothes, nappies, wipes etc. I started to feel excited about the baby. It was time to put things into perspective. I had had Abi with no home what so ever. I had no income and no money and was in debt up to my eyeballs. This time around I have a home, I have furniture, I have a car, I have an income, I have my girls and I have wonderful friends and my mum back. I started to realise I could do this.

I talked to the midwife about my upsets and my concerns with maybe in the future using my mental health to take the baby away. She confirmed this would not happen and it was just all scare tactics using my mental health against me. Both of my girls had been brought up fine in a loving clean and warm home. I had got this far, why would social services suddenly get involved now when they had never been involved before? I knew she was right.

She did offer me some counselling if needed to help me get over everything but to me I didn't feel I needed it. I no longer had anything to be sad about. I have my kids and to me that's all I need. I will love this new baby just as much as my girls and I swear I will do everything in my power to stay on the right track and do the right thing by my children.

Yes, I still had two grand of debt at this point but thanks to my work and the new army reserve retention bonus I knew I would soon clear it. I am officially going to be debt free in a matter of months. It has been my lifelong dream to owe nothing (well apart from the mortgage and a phone contract). I have worked so hard on this journey since 2008 trying to clean up my life. It has taken me eight long years to get to where I am today; there is absolutely no way I am going to let this upset destroy what I have achieved. I am too strong for that. They always say what doesn't break you makes you stronger and I firmly believe that. For now though, me and my absolutely beautiful girls will prepare for my sons arrival.

CHAPTER 39: MAY/JUNE 2016

I finally received my bonus from work and I decided to pay off the last bit of my credit card but also take my little Amelia to Euro Disney in Paris. I had always wanted to go. My sister had been and loved it and I knew in a few months I would be tied down with my new baby so that meant all holidays were going to be on hold so given that thought I booked it.

Abi was spending the May school holidays with her dad, he had booked the time off to see her so I just booked for myself and Amelia to go. I did feel slightly bad Abi was not coming but I had paid for her to go with boarding school only six months earlier and so I knew she was not missing out. So on Monday 30th May 2016 we got on the plane to Paris.

I had invited Jon (by now we had been apart two months and I had calmed down a little), I thought maybe we could try go and be a family and see if anything can be resolved but to my dismay he replied that he was working and that it wasn't a good idea.

I tried, I told myself.

Deep down I knew he was probably right. A lot had been said on both parts. Nevertheless, this did not stop me making the best of it. I was slightly nervous going to France on my own given the recent terror threats but this would not deter me from making this memory with my toddler. We had an excellent few days. It was extremely tiring for me, being over five months pregnant, as it involved a lot of walking but I am so glad I got to show her Disneyland. It was expensive but worth it. We spent four nights in France and had three full days in the Parks itself (which I definitely think was enough), it rained every single day we were there but this did not dampen my spirits. I had found my smile again. Seeing Amelia's face when she saw all the Disney characters she loved was worth its weight in gold. She was so happy.

The first day she was zooming about all over with excitement that I could not keep up with her. I felt proud that after all these years I had actually managed to take her to Disney and enjoy this moment with her. By mid-afternoon she had exhausted herself and she slept for hours, missing the Disney parade. I had to laugh. It was a good job I had booked park tickets for a few days. She had received spending money from her dad and also my mum, so I let her pick some toys from the Disney shop. She was in her element.

On a night-time we ate and slept, we were both knackered and I knew I had made the right decision not booking the more expensive Disney hotels as we would have missed the evening entertainment anyway due to fatigue.

I will treasure the memory of the five days in Euro Disney, just me and Amelia, forever. It's not that I didn't want Abi there, it's just I think a toddler (3-year-old) really believes in the magic of it all.

I loved it and I loved seeing her so happy.

We arrived home on Friday 3rd June and I knew I only had a week to go until my long weekend in Butlin's. This was something I had originally booked for Jon ten months previously. It was a Science weekend and Jon loved Science. Part of me hoped he would ask to come but I soon realised that was not going to happen because again he was working. That, along with the fact nothing between us had been resolved. Still, at that time I had hoped.

With Jon not coming I agreed Abi could take a friend in his place (after all, she never got to go to Disneyland). It was to be a nice girls' long weekend. To be honest, I enjoyed Butlin's more than I enjoyed Disney. This was just because there was less walking and I had Abi with me too. There was a lot less crowds and without sounding like a stereotypical Brit, everyone spoke English. Due to there being less walking for me, I had more energy on a night and I could attend the evening entertainment which I thoroughly enjoyed. Amelia danced all night and Abi was no bother as she had her friend there to chat to as opposed to bugging me 24/7.

It was a lovely little break and I loved it so much I fully intend on going back later this year once my son is here.

CHAPTER 40: BACK AT HOME

Well, after two lovely breaks away, reality hit. I got home and attended another scan on my own (not because I didn't invite Jon but because he was working again). We had still been arguing recently and I was just so fed up of it. It never seemed to end and had been months of stress. Despite everything, I did miss him. I decided to book an appointment with a local medium to see if I could get any spiritual guidance because I just did not know what to do for the best. He arrived at my house and I anxiously waited to see what he would say.

He told me he could see sorrow over a ring coming off and he thought it was completely over and he can't see us working it out. He told me I need to let go. I held back the tears. He went on to describe how it was like a bomb was dropped on our wedding day and nothing has been the same since.

He also said he can see a third person involved and this is why we are arguing. He said he can't see my husband coming back as his loyalties lie with his daughter (I have known this since the day after the wedding). I was told from spirit that I am not to believe this fall-out was my fault (something I have thought and thought about for months).

I was also told to prepare for a messy divorce if things were not sorted. He told me he sees me moving not long after the birth of my son and that I will be hanging up my army boots for good (very true, I had decided not to go back to the army after maternity leave due to childcare costs).

I was told the spirits were around Abi that fateful night and are still around her now, helping her through this life. I just hope this is true and she doesn't end up making the same mistakes as me. He told me whatever I end up doing I will succeed because failure is not an option.

Above all, he told me I am blessed.

After the medium left I thought about what he said for ages. I heard him loud and clear that my wedding ring was off, but was it really off for good?

In my heart of hearts, throughout the whole pregnancy I always thought me and Jon would sort it in the end. My inner gut-instinct was always that when our son arrived, things would be okay. I pondered on this for a good week and when I couldn't stand anymore, I got in touch with Jon, I needed to know what he wanted to do. It had gone on long enough.

I nervously asked him if it was worth trying marriage counselling as one last attempt to save our family. He agreed, but also replied with how hurt and angry he still was. This just made me see red. I knew he wasn't entirely to blame (far from it) but I felt I had been through the mill the whole pregnancy. A third pregnancy more or less on my own is not what I had wished or hoped for. I guess that is life.

Every time I went to a scan and saw happy couples hand in hand waiting to see their unborn baby broke my heart. That should be me, I would think. It hurt like hell but I carried on regardless. I got my head stuck into work for another long month in order to take my mind off everything. Jon was clearly not ready to try just yet after his response but I told myself there was hope there that given time we could maybe more forward.

Working part-time meant I had long weekends to myself with the girls so I busied myself with little weekend adventures out to keep me active. I love showing the girls new places and seeing them smile.

I continued this for the duration of July. At the end of July, we took a little trip to a caravan resort in Skipsea, just to help me try and unwind and so the kids got some fresh sea air. But despite all my trips and keeping busy, Jon was always at the back of my mind and I was forever thinking, what if? All the while hoping Jon would see sense and be ready to move forward, but in the end it was me that pushed for us to meet and see how things went.

I knew getting over the hurt of the wedding would always be there with or without him but I would rather be with him than without him so it was up to me to do something to make the change.

I knew how stubborn he was from previous arguments and I just thought, well, if I don't do something now, he will miss the birth of his own son and its only Amelia and the baby that will suffer.

So I contacted him and he agreed he wanted all the arguments to stop and that we should try one last time.

I had previously told him it was over for good numerous times in a rage and I guess he thought there was no point in trying with me. I understood that. Amelia had horrendously missed her dad and it really broke my heart so I was glad he wanted to also try and move forward, not just for me but for the kids. We arranged to meet and spend some time together for the first time in months. It was a start, but most importantly, the arguments had stopped.

I am not sure if he will ever see my side as to why I was so angry and let down with his daughter on the run up to, and at, the wedding, and I will never understand why he never just said anything and why he decided to tell her our drunken private conversation that we had after the wedding where I stupidly vented my opinions to him. I still to this day though feel betrayed. That conversation was very much private. Regardless, I have put all these thoughts at the back on my mind, the anger is very much still there on both parts but I know there is also still love there too so only time will tell if things can be resolved or if we really do need to move on for good.

I have my really low days when I sit and think about it. There is not a day I don't think about the situation but I know my children need me to be strong and that I am. Time heals pain and I hope this is the case for us. We are on a long road to building our relationship up again but we have made a start and I guess that's the main thing. Our son will not be born into a battle but into a house where mistakes in the past were made but hopefully we have both learnt from it. Amelia is happy to see her dad a lot more again and all in all that makes me very happy. She loves him through and through.

We are now into August and I am eight weeks away from my son's birth date and that fills me with excitement. Myself and Jon have bought most things now and we are ready. Jon is now going to be at home for paternity leave and that makes me happy. All of us together celebrating the baby's arrival. Once he goes back to work in the army after the leave I know he only has a matter of months until he leaves for good and so I thoroughly hope we can put this year behind us and start afresh what with his new job in civilian street and our little family unit.

We hope to move into a bigger property next year (maybe the medium got that bit right about me moving after my sons arrival), but for now we are just waiting until he gets released from the Army and until our son is here safe and sound.

Roll on 2017. It's got to be better than the majority of heartache I have felt during 2016.

CHAPTER 41:
IT DOESN'T ALWAYS RAIN ON ME

So through my whole journey from the age of 16 years old I have made friends, lost friends, gained experiences, learnt a lot about myself, hurt people, unhurt people, loved and lost, gained children, got involved with drugs, got clean, travelled, met new faces, seen some sights, been diagnosed with a mental health disorder, tried to battle my mental health disorder alone and in an organisation that does not fully understand it, I have got into trouble (a lot), I have drank a lot, I have contemplated suicide on more than once occasion, I have battled through debt, I have starved, walked miles when I needed to, got over hurdles, hills and trials and tribulations, I have gained a new-found empathy for Charity work, I have lost myself and found myself again, I have lost my mum and got her back again, I have worked on a relationship with my dad, I have found a passion for fitness (it helps stay mentally strong), I have moved more times than I care to remember, I have been absolutely broken to the point I thought there was no return but here I am, here I stay and here I will always be until my children no longer need me.

Looking back, I would maybe make a few changes (those where I have got too drunk and offended people mainly), but everything else I think I needed it to happen so I could learn from it. It has all happened for a reason and I firmly believe I have a lot better things to come. I hope this is the end of my dark days but this is me. I can never say never. For now though, I have too many things to look forward too.

I have started decorating my home ready for the new baby's arrival. I am really enjoying getting it looking nice (although I do need more space, but for now it's manageable), I have never had my own home before (less for a few months with my first husband prior to splitting) so to me this is a dream come true to have my own home and my family as one even if we are a little squashed. To me, it's a small price to pay.

I am no longer going to sit and worry about the future. I have learnt that that gets you nowhere because what will be will be. My gut instinct says things will be okay and so for now I will go with it. I really hope and feel me and Jon will work. Abi is happy in her school, Amelia is happy her dad is back and our son, well, he will just be the icing on the cake for us all. I am still waiting on the outcome of my army compensation for all the hurt I went through back in York and the way it was all handled. I feel this time in York was a massive career stopper. I am not holding my breath on winning this case because this is me, but as I said, what will be will be.

I have fought this far and I will continue to fight every day for what I believe in.

Me and Kati had been back in touch again, texting (it's few and far between but it's a start). I know I have missed her but maybe again the timing is not right to meet up yet. Despite our fall-out, she was with me through my whole journey from drugs to the end of the army and I will never forget that. If we never get fully sorted again then I know I was lucky to have met her and was blessed to have a friend like her when I needed it the most.

I will never ever acknowledge Amelia's sperm donor. To me he is nothing and always will be. Yes, he may have had his full career in the army (something which proved far more important to him than Amelia) but at the end of the day when all is said and done you can't take it with you. I will die with the memory of my children and that is worth far more than anything in this life. When the time is right I may one day tell Amelia about him but for now she has me and her dad and sister and that's all that she needs. It will always be his loss.

I am now in contact with his ex-wife who turns out lives on the same street as I do (we did not do it intentionally) and Amelia is now in contact with her two half-brothers, although she does not know who they actually are, to her they are friends. Both her half-brothers have nothing to do with their dad either due to his lack of ability to be anything but a selfish twat. He has never been there for his sons either and now they are older they have seen what he is like for themselves and made the decision to cut him out. This surely puts into perspective what kind of man he is and what kind of father he is not. I think fate worked its magic there. It's a funny old thing, fate.

Myself and his ex-wife will continue to build a friendship and I couldn't have asked for anything more.

My sister has just moved into her own home with her husband. I am so proud of her. After years of moving around in rented properties she too has done well for herself. I hope one day soon once moved she makes me an aunty. I am ready. She will make a great mother but she just needs to find the confidence to believe she can do it. She is late 20s so she still has plenty of time. My sister is the more sensible one what with buying a house first and then planning. Not like me at all just jumping in at the deep end at 18 years old with nothing to offer my baby. Lesson learnt. My sister will do well no matter what she decides to do. Her and her husband have the strongest bond and I can only envy her, it's all I have longed for. I am so glad she is now settled and her happiness continues to blossom.

I will continue to build a relationship with my mum, life is too short and I am so glad we have regular contact again. In fact, the past few months she has been my shoulder to cry on. I can tell her anything and she understands. Nothing and nobody will ever cause me to fall out with my mum again, I did truly miss her and I am so glad she decided to get in touch just before my wedding. I do now regret the fact she was not there to see me on my special day but looking at the events of the day I think maybe it was just for the best. My mum has done so well for herself and helps many alcoholics recover. She does a lot of counselling work and these days I find myself being at the top of the list. If I ever have a problem she seems to know what to say to help me fix it. She is one strong lady and I have the utmost admiration for her as she too has come through a lot. We have both learnt from our mistakes and it is time to move forward.

My dad is still struggling with his health but seems to be doing better than previous months. He has just bought a massive American camper van and I hope to one day soon go on a little adventure in it. My dad had been quite supportive through my break-up with Jon over summer and if anything, it has brought us a bit closer. He messages me all the time to see how I am coping and if everything is okay and so I can only be grateful for that.

My brother (my dad's son) is doing really well with work and college. He beat me to it with getting the motorbike license but I am happy for him. I am proud of him, he has done really well for himself and he has turned out a great lad (credit to his mum). Maybe once this baby is out I will continue with my motorbike lessons. For now though, I am happy using four wheels.

My good friends Clare, Athina and Sheree all like always have been there for me. Athina is busy planning her own wedding next year and I am looking forward to that, the hen do is booked for Marbella and so all I can say is stand by all those going to Marbella in March next year, because us girls will be living it large. Vikki will be back on form.

Sheree has some big travel plans coming up and Clare has just started a new job and is also pregnant with her first baby (I am over the moon for her), she lives for her holidays and is a girl after my own heart. I have known these girls for ten years-plus now and I can honestly say I love them with all my heart.

I am only sorry they have to constantly witness my up and downs but I know they understand and will not disown me.

I need to mention my step dad. He brought me up as his own from the age of 2 to 3 years old until the day we moved and my mum left (I was around ten years old). He still to this day classes me as his daughter and we have never lost touch. It might not have been a bed of roses when I was growing up but this man took me in as his own when he didn't have to. To me that will always earn my respect and I will always be thankful.

I am only sorry I have always seemed to be a pain in the arse. Thank you for everything you have helped me with and bailing me out on more than one occasion, you are a good man and I just hope one day you find love again.

Abi will be turning 14 around the time the baby is due and I know that once again she will be a massive help to me. She is amazing. Words cannot express how proud I am to call her my daughter. Amelia is excited for her sibling coming although Amelia wanted a little sister and she stills thinks I am carrying a girl. She talks to my tummy and asks for her to hurry up (there is no convincing her, it's a boy). She thinks in order for me to get the baby out I need to be sick. It makes me laugh. Children are so beautiful and innocent I just wish life as we grow older didn't take that away.

Jon, well, he knows I will always be grateful for the opportunities he gave me. Without him I would never have found the courage to follow my dream and leave the army to make a better, more stable life for my children. I certainly would not have had the time to write this book if I carried on in the army full time. For that I will always be thankful.

Despite all our ups and downs, his heart is in the right place and although his emotional sensitivity to my needs could do with some work, I can't fault him on his work ethics. He will not stop until he knows his family are all provided for. He will always put bread on the table and pay the bills and I guess I can only admire him for that as there are a lot of men out there that have not bothered to work a day in their life.

He worries constantly he's not providing enough to the point it frustrates me but in the grand scheme of things I could have married a lot worse. We are working on our future as man and wife and in time he will learn my ways and I'll learn/get used to his.

When all is said and done, I love him, and that's all anyone needs to know for now.

Thank you to Spiritualism, because in my deepest darkest moments it has somehow always pulled me through. That horrible fateful night where I was ready to leave this world, something stopped me.

I will always believe it with my whole heart.

I do not expect people to understand it nor to believe it, but I know what I believe. I will always believe that that night way back in 2007, someone up there was looking out for me.

It was not my time.

Throughout my journey I have turned to Spiritualism. I always talk to my granddad and I believe in some way or another he is listening and guiding me. I use crystals, tarot and regular medium meetings to help guide me through life. I could not manage without it. It will always be a big part of me and my life and I am so glad I found something that helps me heal.

It has brought me light in the dark and it has brought me inner strength when I had nothing left. I hope to progress this spiritual journey as I grow older.

I always trust my gut instinct with everything now, if it doesn't feel right then that's because it probably isn't!

Through the love of spiritualism and Bon Jovi's good music, I can always get through anything.

I need to thank my current unit, 299 Parachute Squadron in Wakefield. Although they did not know the absolute mess I was in in 2008 when I initially joined the army, I do realise that without using them as a stepping stone back into the Regular Army then I most probably would not be here today. I feel I will always owe them a lot. I never ever meant to use this unit but I am glad I did, it saved my life. I again need to thank them for taking me back seven months ago after leaving the Regular Army, this enabled me to have a smooth transition from Regular to Reserve Forces.

I hope to stay with this unit for a long time. Once again they have given me a chance and it has stopped me going back to being jobless. I will continue to work with them until maternity leave. For everyone there who has taken the time to get to know me and listen to me and to just be there with a daily smile, I just want to thank you. It is a fab unit and if I could erase my blip at Christmas then I would. Onwards and upwards though. There are two ladies there (they know who they are) and without their daily chats I would have crumbled when Jon and I split. I just want to thank you.

I am really enjoying my time at this unit and when all is said and done I will be sad at the end of August when I leave to go on maternity leave.

I know reading this story it looks like I mainly just fall out with people. I just want to reiterate the struggles people suffering with a mental illness have.

It is very hard and will always be a daily struggle to make and maintain relationships. I hope this has come across in my book.

When I am challenged or I do not like something I do not handle it as well as people without anxiety/mood swings would.

I try too but the littlest thing can be a massive hurdle to someone who cannot think it through logically.

Yes, Amelia's biological sperm donor left but I cannot blame myself in the entirety for that, he was still married and leading a double life.

Yes, I fell out with my boss in York but I never asked him to treat me like that. I went to York extremely positive and left feeling broken.

With reference to my mum, this was a silly mistake and we are back on track. Nobody is perfect. If people say they lead perfect life's and do not get angry or face obstacles along the way, then they are lying. Nobody gets through this life unscathed. I have been honest about by troubles. The only fall-out I feel sad about now is my fall-out with my husband. I cannot believe I let someone else come between us to the point it effected Amelia and our unborn son. I will always feel bad for the long five months of upset Amelia endured without her dad, but I cannot dwell on it.

In general, I don't want to sound like a complete and utter ogre because most days I am actually a very smiley and bubbly character. There is so much to live for and so the only way to move forward is to let go of anger. It's hard, but I am doing it (well, I'm trying too).

I will rise above and carry on regardless.

Watch this space.

REVIEW

When you feel like you have nothing left, when you feel like you are on the brink of despair, when the world around you seems not worth living in, then just stop.

Really look at yourself and try and see the world through a child's eyes.

Where everything is so innocent.

Everything is so funny and everything is so beautiful.

Sometimes we just need to be reminded of the beauty that is all around us but we fail to see it in our everyday busy adult lives. I nearly threw my whole life away because of a broken mind. I found a way to fix it. I found a way to help myself. It might have been wrong using the army but rightly or wrongly I am now still here to see my children grow up.

I am so glad I continued with my training when I was ready for death, I am so glad I found the courage to get to the top of the hill when my body was physically ready to give up. The mind is a powerful thing and it was mind over matter. I knew this and I would not let some instructor screaming at me to move my sorry arse, wear me down. I knew I had to keep on running, I am so glad I did.

I am now here to tell my story.

Things could have been very different. I might not be perfect but deep down I have a good heart, I did not do what I did to hurt anyone, nor did I want to use the army but I saw it as an easy way out of corruption. I may dislike the army in some ways now (I've outgrown it and it's served its purpose, the system also let me down when I really needed it) but at the time it saved me from own self-destruction.

I absolutely love life again now. I am almost debt free (down to my last two thousand); I have another child on the way and my two beautiful daughters. I have my own home (it's by no means anything fancy, but it's mine), my own furniture and my own family.

I will never be alone again.

I will fight on every single day to ensure I give my daughters and new baby son the best start in life possible. I will never leave them, I will never let them get hurt and I will never watch them needlessly suffer. God help the first person that ever picks on them because I will come down on them like a tonne of bricks. I am a mother and a friend but most of all I am here, and I always will be.

Well, unless God thinks otherwise.

My next chapter in my life is all happy times. We have holidays to go on, clothes to buy together, cinema trips and theatre trips to go on, hills to walk, restaurants to visit, bike rides to go on, swimming clubs to join, sports trips to accomplish, school exams to pass, first driving tests to go on, first dates to get through, love dilemmas to face, new furniture to buy, first proms to go to, wedding dresses to look at, summer parties to have, new jobs to get through, tough decisions to make, the dangers of drink and drugs to discuss, new houses to look at, gigs to attend, new friends to make, first snogs to get through, first naughties to get through and lots of new beginnings, and all this as a team.

I will be right by their side (not literally in some cases, ha ha!). My children will never be alone, but also now with my lovely family, I have created a team that means I will never ever be alone again.

I am right here, right now, I am me and I am complete.

With thanks to:

My Girls: Abi and Amelia - I owe you my life. If I could give you the world then I would. There are not enough 'Thank you's in this land for you two. You deserve so much more. I am so proud of you both. I hope one day I will make you both so proud of me too. For now all I can do is try and make you smile and love you within every inch of your life. Without you two beauties, I would be merely a nothing. You made me complete again.

My Husband: I understand our 3 years together were not the easiest, circumstances always made it hard for us and it always seemed to provoke a fight. Regardless though I have always loved you. You took on Amelia from a young age and see her as your own, this will always be commendable. You have my respect for that. You helped me follow my dreams to freedom. When we are not tearing shreds out of each other I have always known there is love there. I have always just wanted you to be happy. I know we can move forward and have a bright future. I hope we fulfil our dreams as a team.

John (Abi's dad) – There are no words to describe your loyalty. Without you, I would never have made it. Despite my up and down moods you have always remained my friend. You are a perfect dad to our daughter and a man I really admire and respect. Thank you for being there. I would trust you with my life always. I will always always class you as one of my best most trusted friends.

My sister: You have put up with a lot from me. We were separated at a young age but I always knew I could pick up the phone. You always know what to say to help me and have always been there when it mattered most. You have always been the more adult one out of us both and looked after me more than I have you. I will always be grateful. You and you alone know the struggles we had at the beginning but thanks to you always listening to me, I am here to the end. I love you.

My Mum: I know you blame yourself for leaving. Please be at peace now. I do not blame you for my own choices as an adult. Yes I struggled but who hasn't? I am glad we are talking again and I really missed you when we fell out. I am so proud of you for coming out the other end and overcoming your own battles; you fought your demons and are now strong. I admire all the work you do to help others and you really are an inspiration to those who have battled an illness. The girls and I and soon new grandson will love you always. Thank you for finding the strength to stay on this earth and overcome your struggles. We would be lost without your sound advice now.

Clare, Athina and Sheree: My true friends. Your loyalty to me has not gone unnoticed. At times I feel unworthy to have friends like you. You are my inspirations to keep on going when times are tough. You know me better than I know myself and are always willing to drop everything to help me. I cannot thank you enough. I have nothing to give you back but my love. Know this I will always be there for you all and will love you all forever. Thank you for being my friend.

Jon's Mum: A massive thank you to you for always helping with Amelia and still keeping in touch with her despite the fall out with your son. Lovely lady. You have always made me feel welcome into the family and I thank you for that. Amelia will always see you as a Nanna and I thank you from the bottom of my heart for all you have done for her.

Last but not least, a massive thank you, to my readers. Without you, this book would be merely sat on a shelf being unread. I hope my story opens your eyes to the struggle that is life but also to the fact that you can overcome even the darkest of moments. If I have ever had the pleasure of meeting any of you and you are still a friend now then I really cannot thank you enough for not disowning me, unfriending me or judging me. I love you all.

Peace..............

A bit about my mental health condition:

How common is bipolar disorder?
About 1 in every 100 adults has bipolar disorder at some point in their life. It usually starts between the ages of 15 to 19 - and it rarely starts after the age of 40. Men and women are affected equally.

What types are there?
Bipolar I
- If you have had at least one high or manic episode, which has lasted for longer than one week.
- You may only have manic episodes, although most people with Bipolar I also have periods of depression.
- Untreated, a manic episode will generally last 3 to 6 months.
- Depressive episodes last rather longer - 6 to 12 months without treatment.

Bipolar II
- If you have had more than one episode of severe depression, but only mild manic episodes – these are called 'hypomania'.

Rapid cycling
- If you have more than four mood swings in a 12-month period. This affects around 1 in 10 people with bipolar disorder, and can happen with both types I and II.

Cyclothymia
- The mood swings are not as severe as those in full bipolar disorder, but can be longer. This can develop into full bipolar disorder.

What causes bipolar disorder?
We don't understand this well, but research suggests that:
- Bipolar disorder runs in families - it seems to have more to do with genes than with upbringing.
- There may be a physical problem with the brain systems which control our moods - this is why bipolar disorder can often be controlled with medication.
- But - mood swings can be brought on by stressful experiences or physical illness.

But some people experience feelings of anxiety or depression or suffer mood swings that are so severe and overwhelming that they interfere with personal relationships, job responsibilities, and daily functioning. These people may be suffering from an anxiety disorder, bipolar disorder, or both.

It is not uncommon for someone with an anxiety disorder to also suffer from bipolar disorder. Many people with bipolar disorder will suffer from at least one anxiety disorder at some point in their lives.

Suffering from an anxiety disorder and bipolar disorder has been associated with decreased functioning and quality of life and an increased likelihood of substance abuse and suicide attempts. Insomnia, a common anxiety disorder symptom, is a significant trigger for manic episodes

I can confirm I was diagnosed with Cyclothymia. Not quite as severe as Bipolar disorder but still a Mood Disorder that very much affects my everyday life. It is a constant daily struggle. I do not take medication for it (not just because I am pregnant), this is due to my own choice.

I feel I can manage it better now. I know when I am going on a downward spiral or rant and I know how to cope with it slightly better. The worst thing for me to do is drink alcohol when I feel angry. Even if I have the tiniest gripe, I cannot drink because if it's not sorted and I drink, well, it's like unleashing a red flag to a bull.

I have learnt this lesson and I will never drink again when even the slightest bit mad. It's not worth it. It has cost me relationships and friendships. I know when a low spell is coming on that I need to go out, even if it's just for a walk. Exercise does help.

I try to eat healthy; healthy body, healthy mind (well, sometimes). When I am over-happy or giddy, my eldest daughter usually lets me run about the house like a headless chicken until it's out of my system. If anything, it makes her laugh.

Bottom line is, I am coping!

I try really hard to keep busy all the time so I don't have to deal with my low moods when they arise, most of the time I am knackered because of this reason, but I do not want to risk sitting and over-thinking because that's when I get in a low mood state and it's so hard to clutch my way out of it.

Hopefully, as time goes on I can manage it more with experience, but for now I will continue to keep busy and focused on my children, I find that just about gets me through anything.

Made in the USA
Charleston, SC
21 September 2016